Down The Rabbit Hole
The Curious Case of Innovation
Jane La Mantia de Pencier

Edited by Neil Seeman

Health Strategy Innovation Cell
Massey College, Toronto

www.innovationcell.com

Published by Bounce!
curiousinnovation@gmail.com
Copyright © 2010 Jane La Mantia de Pencier

ISBN 978-0-9867955-2-7 (paperback)

With thanks to Neil Seeman, Carlos Rizo, JoAnn Purcell and Adam de Pencier.

Innovation?

This small volume is a collection of thoughts about a topic which has become pivotal in these first years of the 21st century; in name, it is innovation. As a word it is grossly overused and ill-defined. As a notion it is opaque, moveable and only comprehensible within the genre or social compartment in which it is coined. As an ideal, it folds back onto the basic notions of humanity like truth, beauty, clarity, value, and even a search for godliness.

If you are looking for definitive answers this is not the place to find them. If you are looking for flow charts and evidence based discussion, this collection may cause you frustration. If you think you can tolerate a pixilated view of our world in which a Van Gogh haystack is a collection of colours and textures, or the identity of a Dégas dancer becomes inseparable from the otherworldliness of her tutu, you might be able to tolerate this much lesser attempt at revealing something to ourselves, in words, not paintbrushes, of our current cultural obsession. This is a collection of thoughts about innovation, which I'm hoping are interesting both individually and as a whole. I like to think there is a larger message created in them as a set.

On a personal note, I've been working with the Health Strategy Innovation Cell at Massey College in Toronto. The Cell is thinking about the healthcare experience and what is revealed in online patient conversations, which are increasingly happening in real-time. Somewhere in the online message may be the seed of a positive and disruptive healthcare innovation. For me, this schooling in the world of healthcare policy has come with a steep learning curve. For a while I've been wondering about the degree to which I'm suited or interested in the task, and this was exacerbated while attending a series of healthcare tradeshows and symposia at the Metro Toronto Convention Centre.

Across a huge floor, row upon row of healthcare industry exhibitors set up booths. Gussied up tables lined aisles of green carpet and crushed faux grass. Exhibits boasting charts and graphs, tables of data and arrows leading from this finding to that dominated the room. All paths of thinking were exhibited with a self-congratulatory clarity and were designed to show as little waste as possible in both mind and material. The room was filled with data and connectors while white fold-up tables modeled the latest trade-show fashions with paid-by-the-hour attitude.

The thinkers in the booths seemed earnest and committed to their work. They were not so glamorous people with clips and clipboards. Sure, I understood each individual had a history and enjoyed an orbit that was rich, colourful and profoundly their own, and yet as a group they seemed like starry-eyed Believers. They appeared indistinct and without aesthetic. They seemed as if they had found Truth and were eager to tell it.

I was disturbed. I was maybe even a little freaked out. Why? What could possibly be the matter with me? Why did the scene make my heartbeat fast, and why was my stride stiff and unnatural? I'll tell you why. I was scared. It looked like systems had overtaken thinking. Form was king. I'd had this particular fright while working in the corporate world. I've had this feeling waiting in doctors' offices. I've had this feeling when filling out necessary questionnaires for certain applications or evaluations. What could possibly be so scary? Artlessness can. It is gossamer scaled with gills pumping begging for aesthetic while tail fins beat causing it to flip-flap on a rock. It makes a person want to rush to the rescue, but where can it be tossed? There is no wet homage to beauty in sight. There is only tidiness and an outdated etiquette of design which brings a large plant on the scene with an enormous plastic purple bow. Die fish die.

I looked at my colleagues from the Cell. They appeared enthusiastic and energized by the displays. I was not. What could I possibly bring to this equation? I was definitely a different kind of thinker. My colleagues knew this and they seemed willing to tolerate my presence. They were even welcoming. That's pretty open-minded, I thought. I wanted to learn from them, and from my position as a bit of a fly in the soup. So, even as I stood askance, I was intrigued.

"What about all the important stuff and ideas between the lines," my psyche screamed!

Don't get me wrong. I find organization immensely satisfying. I hunger for a place for this or that thing. I aspire to labeling the boxes of my life from seasonal decorations to tax receipts. I enjoy a certain cautious delight in the compartmentalization of thought. However, in the way I live from day to day and on the subject of health, body, happiness and prosperity I'm looking for systems that envelop a broad world view, rather than systems which delineate one. At the health conventions, a kind of world was being expressed that seemed incompatible with this. Policy makers, "knowledge-transfer" specialists, biomedical and bio-device salespeople stood shoulder to shoulder. Pharmacological industry executives swooped in and around looking for an ear, while the manager of the industry for the latest stretcher or patient identification device handed out pens and hand-sanitizer. GE Healthcare offered pedometers and I strapped mine on instantly. I counted my steps, thinking.

I walked, thinking. When a singer is learning an operatic role there are many ways she approaches the challenge. It is a step-by-step process for most people, and it usually begins with metre. The singer counts out the role. The singer may speak through the score using the time signatures, "1 & 2 & 3 a-half-a 4." Then she may add the words speaking them out loud to the rhythm. If she knows the language she won't have to go into a step of translation, but she may have a step which does involves translation, diction and comprehension. She needs to understand the characters and motivation like any actor. This requires time and attention to detail. It requires efficiency because preparation time, as in any business, is usually limited. Learning the music often comes last. Listening to the aesthetic clues the composer offers in the score and instrumentation is necessary fine tuning. Interpretation makes the artist.

All of these steps, and they do vary, are essential to the performance. So, as a person who's had some very small experience in this area, I understand the need to compartmentalize, work efficiently, and build on systems. The world's finest performers excel at the steps. The process, though, is not enough. The steps exquisitely executed do not create the world's greatest singers on their own. Leaving voice quality out of the equation and just supposing it is of celestial origin, a consummate completion of the tasks is not enough to create a singer who elevates the listener in the experience.

The singers who transport the listener bring more to music than the building blocks. Yes, these singers bring a whole, made up of the parts. The parts might still be discernible, a bit like the impressionist's brush stroke, in that they remain somewhat individuated and stylized. The singer who is a wonder is capable of making the whole greater than the parts. She brings a life force to the collection of pieces, and the relationship with the listeners, too, becomes integrated into the creation. The listener becomes a participant in the performance.

The green carpet in the convention hall buckles up here and there. I walk and ponder this particular imperfection caused by the application of people to the venue. I walk, not tripping. So, how does the opera singer's method apply to the world of healthcare? Just like the singer on the stage, the front line performance of the healthcare professionals should not be confused with the methodology that comes before the clinical relationship. As long as the patient is fully involved in their healthcare experience, all the flow charts, tables and data crunching should act not as a hindrance but as a tool for building excellent healthcare.

"Calm down, Jane," I admonish myself.

The thing about good singers, though, is that not all singers are that good, and not all singers have the breadth, sensitivity or ability to engage an audience in a profound manner. Not all listeners are capable of lending themselves to the aesthetic process. It is the same in the health world. Some doctors are brilliant at pulling the pieces together. Some lock these pieces together rigidly. Others leave space in the components of their medical education to allow for inflow of information and the shifting of assumptions. Really good doctors are probably like the rare singer, and draw the patient into the flow of the thinking. Really good patients engage with their doctors. I stopped walking and witnessed sheer celebration at the "Information Systems" booth. There, a machine was spitting treatment labels into the hands of enthusiastic emergency room administrators. "clickety...click, click, click."

So, as I looked at my GE Healthcare pedometer and the patient-labeling pandemonium, I was reminded that foundations on which to build a craft are not to be feared. It is only when the foundations become the end to the experience that trouble is afoot. It is equally worrisome when the foundations are rigid. The first tremor snaps them. The healthcare conferences may have represented rigidity and they may not have. The reality of that is in what happens outside the big convention centre and between the caregivers and the patients and their access to each other.

Innovation needs to be considered as a collection of pieces that come together to make a whole, like the impressionist painting. The components that create it are highly varied and subjectively selected, but it might be fun to experiment with these. It's not clear which ones are primary. Do personal themes dominate universal themes? Maybe Van Gogh always started with blue, or maybe he followed the colours of the spectrum: red, orange, yellow, green, blue, indigo and violet.

Ahead are the categories into which I've attempted to think about innovation. I'm hoping the collection breathes and I know the participation of the reader is essential. These categories can be shaken up, or entirely different. The goal is to separate out some colours with which to paint. As, Jascha Rushkin, my ninety-four year old singing coach used to say, "after you've mixed the colours on your palette, it's up to you to use them."

So what follows are four categories or colours with which I'll paint an image of innovation. Let's see what comes.

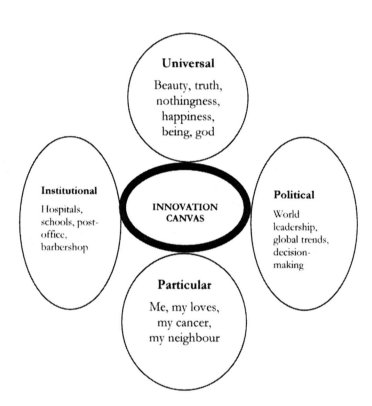

Universal

Beauty, truth, nothingness, happiness, being, god

Institutional

Hospitals, schools, post-office, barbershop

INNOVATION CANVAS

Political

World leadership, global trends, decision-making

Particular

Me, my loves, my cancer, my neighbour

Table of Contents

Introduction

Universal

Particular

Institutional

Political

Conclusion

UNIVERSAL

What is Innovation?

What is this recurring reference to innovation? It has become a fad. It's getting on my nerves. Sure, I'm irritable. Perhaps I need a little Valerian or St. John's Wort, an SSRI, or meta-amphetamine.

Everywhere you go someone is declaring something innovative, from pepper grinders to bras with memories, from musical styles to cars with attitude. Is the idea of innovation somehow distinct from anything new? Is innovation simply about the next model? Is innovation a change of any kind? Do I want my bra to have a memory?

Change can happen by accident. Can innovation happen by accident? Mutations are accidents and some of them have been monumental. Is there negative innovation? I don't think so.

Innovation is positive

It has been suggested to me that innovation is always about utility. An innovation is something with material application, it was said. Anything innovative is a tool or a device. At time of writing the Health Strategy Innovation Cell analytics reveal 1.1 million tweets and 32.3 million web hits where the word innovation appears alongside terms that have a utilitarian smell. The terms are pretty ordinary and seem to lack big ideas. It all wafts mercantile to me. It fills me with apocalyptic thoughts about the quality of our liberal education and the vacuity in our collective spirituality. Innovation can't be just about tangibles and business models. Can it? Aren't some ideas innovative, even really esoteric ideas that maybe have no utility in themselves, but that point in a new direction? A method can be innovative.

A useful take-away from the idea of "innovative" might be the implied connectivity. Innovation comes out of or into something else. Innovation is, while part of a continuum, something that establishes a new trajectory for the particular idea, thing, or process? If I engage a Google™ search for innovation continuum I find 1.28 M entries, innovation and continuum, 1.27 M and for "innovation continuum" the result it 23,000.

Those numbers are rather low in World Wide Web terms. I wonder why the continuum is not more discussed. Could there be something learned from acknowledging the continuum or denying the continuum? What is disruptive innovation?

The Power of Bounce

A new idea owns a particular trajectory as does the old idea, or sameness, partake of a trajectory or direction of energy. If the new idea hits the status quo and is a more powerful force, there will be a bounce and everything will adopt a new direction.

Bounce? Well, how is something put on a new course? According to physical laws, once in motion, anything expends all of its energy maintaining that direction and it actually takes a collision of sorts, an influx of energy from a different vector, to bump the thing onto a new path

Innovation is an action

Energy is something that is neither created nor destroyed. Energy can neither grow nor be spent. Energy will necessarily collide with anything in its path. To create a bump the incoming energy has to be greater than the force, or in the case of this conversation, the idea with which it is colliding. If it is more influential it will send thinking off in a new direction. If it is greater it will also gain and be reinforced by that with which it has collided. It will increase. It will become more powerful. If it has less energy it will be absorbed into the greater entity or idea and that idea will prosper. Innovation is a force that is stronger than the status quo and is fed by the status quo.

What determines whether there will be a collision? Is it random? Does it come from chaos and a chaotic characteristic of our world? Is it from the opposite, order, and a tendency of things to fall into order? Is there energy in order? Well, yes, but maybe that energy is all expended in maintaining the order. This is entropy. Sounds a bit like housekeeping. So, maybe in entropy there is no energy available for creation or innovation because in a system of order there are no happy collisions. Maybe excessive order is found in times of stillness like the dark ages and entrenched high maintenance hairstyles.

Bertrand Russell commented on the subject of order and house-keeping. He said something like, "There can be no higher thinking without domestic help". To be sure, he was of a different age. He liked a servant or two. He may also have been observing the struggles of his friend and poet Robert Graves.

Graves had a pile of children, and not only was he weighed down by the need of an income, he was distracted in his physical space in a small and messy cottage. He couldn't write. He was too busy with the kids, the debt and the general domestic chaos. His friends, particularly T.E. Lawrence helped out by sending him a wallop of the proceeds of *Seven Pillars of Wisdom*. In fact he gave him four chapters to serialize in the United States. This helped with Graves' debts and helped him establish order in his house. He hired a housekeeper. It seems he needed order and he needed the burden of maintaining it to be met by someone else.*

Russell, in his book, *In Praise of Idleness* wrote about the labours of women in the home. He saw that a life spent in sustaining the banal material order of a household could crush the energy, creativity and innovation of a mind. Energy spent maintaining order is audible. It's the great cacophonic suck of entropy. You can hear it sometimes. At least, I can, when I'm vacuuming.

Does innovation require a messy house, or a house in which others, who harness dirt as their business, do the dust ball wrangling? Does innovation require freedom from order or just order's maintenance? Does innovation require chaos? Does innovation require leisure?

Innovation comes from chaos, from accident and the random fluctuations of the universe. Chaos and order are perhaps necessary to each other a lot like hills and valleys. Innovation would mean nothing without stasis. Intersecting lines are more fun than parallel lines but necessary to each other for the very stuff of their relevance. This suggests that all innovative times require dull times. Dark ages seem important. How dark do things have to get? How dark is it now?

Are we ready for a whole new world? Are we ready for a little bit of a new world? Does innovation come in little bits?

*(Alice Munro is said to have written some of her finest work at her dining room table with her children running all around and chaos prospering.)

Innovation and Beauty

Is the innovative sometimes embracing what is staid? Are we so progress-fixated that it would be innovative to reject new ways and embrace the old? We could seek out the ugliest clothes, the uglier the better, drive big gas guzzling cars that spew as much exhaust as possible. We could frequent deep-fried hormonally laced chicken restaurants while wearing a full mask of flesh coloured make-up. We could then rinse off the chicken grease in the nearest lake with lots of shampoo and run motor boats in circles over breeding grounds. I guess we won't do that.

What in our thinking guides us away from this sort of behaviour? Most of us really don't want to do these things? Is it virtue? Vanity? I think we understand the obvious reason for not doing these things, but I think we overlook the aspect of our human condition that makes it impossible for us to continue in certain ways. Human beings necessarily move toward beauty. We try to figure out where beauty is and, when we think we know, we move toward it.

Is there a chance that the search for the innovative is in following the ever-moving light that is beauty? Beauty seems to be the firefly or the beacon of light we seek. We try to put it in a jar whether it is an ideological beauty or another kind of beauty. Perhaps, beauty is the guide to innovation, and if we acknowledge this, we'll find some sort of way to anticipate where innovation will appear, or maybe better, what changes are truly innovative and what ideas are mistakes. We recognize a little bit of ugliness in mistakes. This comes down to an inextricable link between truth and beauty? This would suggest innovation is truth or the path toward truth. Perhaps so, in that it represents an earnest motion toward an ideal. Maybe that's why the fun is over once the firefly is in the jar. The chase is finished.

Wait a minute. What explains ugliness in the world? Why do some people seek out horror stories and violent sports? Why is there systematic torture? For some, this is entertainment. These are trivial and fleeting games for the perpetrators. Even the worst despots and practitioners of cruelty have been notorious for juxtaposition of character. Often, their most vain and urgent pleasures have grown out of their sense of beauty in art, architecture, landscape, design, music, and their vision of a perfect innovative world.

Trust, Innovation and Humility

There's a lot of talk about trust these days. It's mostly about money. Can we trust the banks, the stock broker or the realtor? It's also about health. Why get a test? The results are unreliable. Why get a test? My doctor won't look at the results.

Do you trust your doctor? What is trust? When is the element of trust brought in to any relationship? It's about vulnerability. We feel compelled to trust when we are looking for something. Sometimes we are just looking for a higher level of meaning in a relationship. We don't want to have secrets and we think that by trusting, revealing our vulnerable side, we will enhance the depth of the commitment to another. Sometimes we feel compelled to trust when we need the assistance of another.

We trust a broker with our investment dollars because that broker or bank can do something with our equity that we cannot. They can take our money and grow it to a quantity that will serve us in the future. We think.

Trust and Vulnerability in the Doctor's Office

What about the trust with which we initiate a relationship with a doctor? We present ourselves in our most vulnerable condition to another individual. We participate in a formulaic relationship that says: because this person has a certain accreditation we will find help from him or her, and they will not violate our trust. There is more than one way for trust to be violated but for the sake of moving along let's just pretend that a violation of trust is understood.

Trust and Financial Engineering

In the financial world, trust imploded when the entire system broke down. Incompetence or rapaciousness or a bit of both led to widespread suffering. This led to a new age of skepticism. Is there a similar breakdown occurring in healthcare? Has the patient lost trust in the system? Has the patient lost trust in the doctor? Are we simply in an age where the patient is more informed and is expecting the healthcare professional to communicate with them on a more sophisticated level? When the professional proves ill-equipped to do so, does trust break down? The communication problems might suggest a deficiency in professional training. Perhaps medical schools need to establish new ways of training a doctor to deal with a new age of medicine. Are the schools still teaching a pre-knowledge, pre-electronic age of patient interaction?

Perhaps the healthcare system is crumbling in a new electronic age in just the way the financial world could not keep up with technology as noted by Nassim Nicholas Taleb. The author refers to the Blackberry™ impact on information gaps that had, prior to the launch, allowed a window for speculative trade. With the advent of the Blackberry, the buy and sell timing window disappeared. Those brief seconds of an information void, where status of trade was a mystery and speculative trading was covered in darkness, was suddenly revealed. That's one reason the crash happened so fast. Once the light went on there was no hiding the leveraging. Maybe this closing of the information gap is also affecting healthcare.

The Promise of Humility to Close the Trust Gap

Maybe the health professional is not equipped to address the concerns of the newly knowledgeable patient. Perhaps the only way any human being can function in this knew all-knowing age is to act in partnership from a position of humility. Doctors who admit ignorance when they don't know an answer will be trusted by a knowledgeable patient. In years gone by doctors were trained to inspire a sort of awe, and thus gain the confidence of patients. Part of the rationale for this was that it would be comforting for the patient to think that the doctors knew what they were talking about. Most patients now have a more sophisticated understanding of medical process. The age of posturing just might be over.

Trust is important in any professional relationship and in any important human interaction. Healthcare professionals need to nurture this. Patients need to expect this and actively participate in its creation. Healthcare systems need to earn it through good governance, policy and oversight and, most effectively, through the ongoing work of good people.

Healthcare and The Salons of France

Sitting in my garden watching a squirrel flow over and under fences with no acknowledgement of a barrier, other than the navigational one, I'm thinking of that critter's open source attitude. He seems to be of the mind that all is available to him and it's available for his use and sustenance.

In my hands, I have Simon Schama's *Citizens: A Chronical of the French Revolution*, and I'm thinking about how the salons of Paris in the late 1700s compare to the birth of the World Wide Web and even to the Innovation Cell of which I'm a part.

I guess it's pretty obvious. It's all about sharing transformative ideas and collaboration and evolving to a new social place. Maybe the last notion needs to be highlighted in a definition of innovation. Maybe innovation is not just about newness: it's also about evolving.

By the 1770s, Schama writes, the attendance at the Salon Carré of the Louvre was a "huge boiling soup of humanity." It's all described by a journalist of the time in the most florid language of disgust about the shoulder to shoulder odour and filth. The journalist found the lesser classes smellier than the noble, but something tells me, they were all rather malodorous. They stuck around wafting up their personal fumes and talking about all sorts of things. Schama writes about the "forming of a single public" as people of all classes partook in the discussions. There were elite salons, too, where an invitation was required and coveted, and where a young intellectual might be the star attraction amongst a bunch of older established types.

Rousseau had a good time enjoying the chocolate mousse at these thinkery soirées. There was debate. There was also the ignition of something powerful, maybe curiosity. Sure, that whole French exercise moved toward the problematic. The revolution was unrelenting and brutish. Many of the artists who had discovered a new voice in this milieu were most active in its dismantling. Apparently the poets and the clowns, the playwrights, acrobats and painters became some of the most effective citizens in the rounding up of necks for that killing machine, the innovative guillotine. Now that's a rock in the blade of the idea that innovation is always positive.

Yes, innovation sometimes comes in a raucous fashion. Things started out looking pretty festive in France with the big social mix. All classes of society enjoyed watching hot air balloons and street festivals. They enjoyed the discussion and ideas, but once the people of all classes became more informed and started to communicate with each other, they wanted more in their daily lives. They wanted liberté, égalité, fraternité. Well, it's hard to argue with that. Those are really pretty good things to strive for and that's what the World Wide Web offers now. We all have access to a wide swath of real-time information. It's available to us instantly. We're seeking it out, and with it we're conversing with a social network from around the world. It is, indeed, world-wide.

Healthcare and liberté, égalité, fraternité

Healthcare has been informed by this new age of information. We want our healthcare experience to be better, perfect even. We want liberté, égalité, fraternité. Many of us want to be informed about our maladies and possible treatments before we show up in the doctors' offices. We want our doctors to engage in a discussion with us about our illness. Maybe we want them to engage in an exploration with us about our situation.

Some doctors find these Web-educated patients difficult. They sometimes have the wrong information or superficial points of view. Increasingly, the patient who walks into a doctor's office is of a new species. The patient on Tuesday who has the same trouble as the patient on Monday may have an entirely different, or an updated, bank of information at his disposal. Availability of information is on a seeming logarithmic expansion, and patients' access to new thinking and community is now instant. While the instant information revealed the flaws in the banking systems the same phenomenon in healthcare does not have to be threatening. It can be used positively. This instant information can be used to make the healthcare experience fantastically efficient, satisfying for a patient with a need to know, and hopefully, effective.

Will the new intellectual salons, online chat rooms, Web sites, or Twitter™ micro-diaries lead to a rising up of people and a great bloody unrest? Will there be a tumultuous revolution of our healthcare system? No, I don't think so, because everyone is a participant. As healthcare workers, patients, government health bodies, insurance and pharmaceutical companies and their distributors all join the conversation we'll be a happy mass of health seeking individuals.

I'll be sitting in my garden imagining an entertaining metaphor for the innovations of our age. The great invention of the late 1700s, the hot air balloon, will open its valves, hiss, plump up and take flight. As it lifts, the garden squirrel will run to the top post of the invisible fence, and in a great flying squirrelly moment, innovate himself aboard. He'll leap.

I'll hold my breath as the massive balloon of our age lifts. I'll cheer as it floats up, higher and higher. My neighbours will hear my celebration. They'll peer through the fence, thinking I've come undone. They'll look to the sky. The balloon will catch the wind. The neighbours will see the ascending balloon. The innovation squirrel will skip along the edge of the basket as he gets smaller and smaller in the sky. All will cheer.

We'll run out to the street and in a great mob chase the balloon as it travels across the sky. Sure it might crash, but that's just the way of innovation, the idea that knowledge should be available to all, and the can-do will-do attitude of the flying squirrel.

Mind, Money and Momentum

The year is 1782. Night after night, and years after that, William and Caroline Herschel worked at their telescopes. Many of their discoveries were a surprise to them. Some came from a studied and methodical mapping of the skies, but the revelations themselves were not willed. They came from a lifetime of dedication and the building of expertise. They came from uncertainty and curiosity. The Herschels experimented and they exhibited a willingness to try things. They needed a lifetime of tinkering and error without regard for financial return. They grew a certain knowledge. They propelled a study, astronomy, in an entirely new direction. They innovated.

Do the realities of our mercantile age make it impossible for people to work away at their passions without the promise of a quick monetary return? William and Caroline Herschel did have a benefactor in the Royal Society led by its President Sir Joseph Banks, and ultimately, from the purse of the apparently crazy King George. Were their times subject to any less financial pressure than ours? Did they need wealth and a kind of fame to continue? Absolutely they did.

A Royal Garden Party at their country laboratory was held to showcase their grand new telescope in the making. It was an investor's showcase if ever there was one. The Duchess of This and the Duke of That with various other members of royal designation all climbed aboard their carriages for the Astronomer's Picnic. It was a jolly day. The hats were big. The smiles were broad. The grinding of the lenses and the tour of the grounds made an excellent backdrop for social intrigue and fun. It was the picnic of the season. So, the king came forward with the loot after the event, but he was miffed. He felt the decision to fund or not to fund had been taken from him by the picnic generated enthusiasm of the Court. The hero astronomers were simply too popular to deny.

Today, leading business consultancies and think tanks are recommending the offering of awards or prizes for innovation. It has become clear to some that innovation in any area requires an extra nudge. They point to the reality that the most risky of ideas, which are sometimes the most innovative, cannot get off the ground because of funding restrictions.

The need for companies to show return to investors or shareholders at year-end makes it very difficult for the average CEO to take risks. If things go wrong they must confront a hostile Board. One proponent of a prize says a "properly structured" prize "...allows for balance-sheet risk taking." Governments can only invest so much in these ventures too, as leaders require re-election and are accountable to the most ordinary-minded of voters. Innovators must be turned into heroes as a public relations exercise. It is necessary for self-preservation.

Sir Joseph Banks understood the hero model as a fundraising tool. Banks was quick to announce and celebrate the Herschels' discoveries of comets, moons, and nebulae. After all, as President of the Royal Society, his reputation was on the line too. Success was essential. The Herschels and Joseph Banks were in a state of high stress when the forty foot telescope financed by King George was slow to produce results.

The King was further agitated. Banks who had the job of reporting directly to the Royal offices was, himself, pressuring the astronomers to produce. The astronomers worked under stress and growing exhaustion. There were all sorts of difficulties with the mirrors, moisture in the glass, the shifting of weights and problems of construction. These all caused waste in the budget and anxiety in the creators.

The Crown and the Royal Society were proud of the Herschel discoveries particularly as they played against the achievements of the Observatoire de Paris. This matter of Empire pride, along with Joseph Banks' hero making picnic, are what helped keep the Herschels financed.

What are the variables that today hold the iron pincers on the purse of research and start-up? Do they spring open on the energy of public pride? Will they release the goods based on promise of financial return? Where do the issues of mind, money and momentum come together today? How tightly are they linked? Was their co-dependence ever thus, and will it ever be? Will mind never be free from the practical notions, outside a well-financed and tenured university model? How do we weigh the value of life's non-utilitarian considerations, the beautifully useless ones, with their very opposite?

There have been many mathematicians who have proudly spouted on about math's uselessness. Those very thinkers, who celebrate mathematics as an end in itself, have provided tools for other people of utilitarian inclination. Maybe a certain social maturity comes with an understanding of the absence of polarities, and the absence of uselessness.

As a society, maybe we have to understand the combination of thought and utility as a human reality. It's a notion that makes the earth quake. Surely there are ideas for ideas sake. Maybe, but once ideas are formed they just flow out into the world. Maybe what we've always seen as separate and, in fact functioning on a higher plane, when purely themselves, are incomplete and still when un-combined. Maybe we just can't help ourselves from being an applied species.

How Place Affects our Thinking

Some friends of mine have been sailing off the isle of Kos. I think that's pretty wonderful and ponder what their days are like. Surely they awaken early, with the water lapping the edge of the boat, the sun shining into the portholes and streaming in a narrow beam down the slightly opened hatch. They hear the fishermen coming back with the catch, whistling and shouting as the day's take is heaved, up, onto the stone docks. They emerge, with hair still wound by the previous day's wind, and look positively Ancient Greek.

Then I remember. Hippocrates was from Kos, Hippocrates who was of the four humours, and so much more. Yes, the four humours were to represent all the fluids of the body: blood, black bile, yellow bile and phlegm. That's a nasty representation of the human self. It's not a description of the person, though. These are the fluids of illness. Well, it wasn't a totally crazy notion. When Hippocrates saw an over-abundance of phlegm he prescribed citrus.

The four humours, the cardinal humours, are drawn out compass style. As is north, south, east, west, so is blood, black bile, yellow bile and phlegm. Did he come up with this notion as a child of Kos? Did it have something to do with living on an island? Did it have something to do with so much dependency on travels by sea? An awareness of the horizon in all directions does much to influence the mind, as any sailor can attest who has looked out on a still sea with no land in sight. Schubert wrote a powerful song to this effect, *Meeres Stille* set to Goethe's poem. It can be terrifying to we mere mortals, as Goethe wrote "Todesstille fürchterlicht!" (Dead calm, terrifying?) Academies of Art are filled with artistic creations inspired by every condition on the oceans.

I wonder if things innovative come from the natural conditions of our lives. Is our ability to think guided by our surroundings? To think in a manner that is clear and fresh, do we have to allow for a certain sensuality or poetry? Does poetry come only from the natural world? Is poetry all about the senses, and is rich ingestion of things empirical necessary to inspire even the most abstract of notions?

When the anchor is pulled and the sailboat moves away from the shore and into the wind, will the compass in its fundamental earthliness inform the sailors aboard that ship in a way that is more than a pointing of the thumb, "that-away"? Will the very basic magnetic properties of this earth, the water on which they travel, the air that blows through their tresses making them look like demi-gods, and the fire in the galley that made the morning coffee help them think of things in a way that is uninformed by banal predispositions of the world? Will it allow them to recreate their world view? Is this from where innovation comes? Does everything innovative ignore assumptions, and charter a course according to the simplest notions and, what seems to be, the magnetically true? Was it necessary to Hippocrates' innovative thinking that he lived on the island of Kos?

Is where we live and how we respire with our environment the very seed of our thinking? Do we need to be willing to engage the most elemental aspects of our earthly selves in order to think afresh?

Images and Our Ability to Understand

What's not working? Globally, millions of people have no access to what we call "modern medicine". We are a species divided on so many fronts. We are a species of too many tribes and too many constituencies. What is the genesis of this? How can it be overcome? The answer to the first question has maybe become uninteresting under the weight of the second. How can this be overcome? The answer may be electronic photo sharing. The answer may be You Tube™ and other visual tools.

Gordon Brown addressed the *TED Talks* audience in July 2009 and pointed to the power of images. We are, after all, empirical people, perhaps more than an intellectual species, and what we see has the power to move us. Mr. Brown shows a few images of our photographic age and points to their power to bring people to action. The image of nine year old Kim Phúc running in physical and emotional pain with her back scorched off in Vietnam, the student standing in front of the tanks in Tiananmen Square, and images of the starving in any number of droughts and famines. He refers to images in the Children's Museum of Rwanda. The Yad Vashem archives offer images to help us understand the Holocaust. The news footage of the 2010 earthquake in Haiti moved people all over the world to take action and give money.

We keep photo albums and buy video cameras. We watch news online and on television. We look to the front page photos on the daily newspaper. We buy a magazine moved to do so by glossy cover images. We are profoundly impacted by the visual. More importantly, we act, based on visual stimuli. Mr. Brown says,

"What we see unlocks what we cannot see. What we see unlocks the invisible ties and bonds of sympathy that bring us together to become a human community."

Maybe it's time for a visual telling of the world's healthcare status. Maybe it's time to show each other our physical struggles. Our healthcare process has always been as private as possible. This is a part of how we interpret human dignity. What if, some generous people such as the cancer sufferer Farrah Fawcett show us their suffering or their recoveries, or their treatments, or their process of dying? Would healthcare reform and innovation come more quickly if we could all see what is going on behind those hospital curtains? How would we distinguish a true representation of a healthcare process from a representation offered by an exhibitionist or a patient with an axe to grind? I don't know. Maybe a good visual editor, just like any print editor, could siphon off the false and bring forward the communicative unbiased and journalistic images.

We could also learn to think about innovation in healthcare as a global concern. We need to think of healthcare innovation globally, and as a responsibility that reaches beyond the zip of the curtain, the rumble of the carts and that unusual smell of food, antiseptic and human secretions that meet in the glamorous and imperfect First World hospital.

Evolutionary Priorities: Fun or Safety?

There is an article in Issue 72 of *Philosophy Now* by anthropologist, Dawn Starin, entitled *Contemplating Colobus*. Dr. Starin, the credits report, has spent the "last few decades studying primates in Africa and Asia." Well, that's pretty interesting, as is her particular voice and the way she seems to process the evidence before her. In Gambia, Dr. Starin watched the Colobus monkeys in their daily behaviour. She noticed something that especially got me pondering as it relates to cognitive biases, mistakes, and innovation.

The monkeys sometimes watch pythons from up high and observe the snakes making tracks on the forest floor. Starin describes the track like a "bald tire tread winding along a dirt road". The tracks are bold and obvious. She even notes that it's easy to identify when the track is fresh. It broadcasts loud and clear: the snake is nearby. The snake is looking for dinner and the Colobus is on the menu. The monkey is well warned and should know to be cautious at the sight of the track. On the contrary, the doctor reports she sees the monkeys playing on the constrictor's path and chasing each other around on the ground.

"Laughing, their eyes shut, the young Colobus roll around on the ground next to and all over the track. The adults sit on the track eating fallen fruit."

She sees no evidence that they've made a connection between the track and the danger. The snake lurks and the monkeys show no caution. Why do they not make the connection between the path and the snake? Why are they not alert to the danger? Where is their fear?

There is a lot of talk lately about randomness and how we often attribute connections when none are valid. We've all made specious connections. Jails are filled with some who may be wrongly convicted. Witches have been burnt at the stake for failing the test of flotation. If they sank and drowned they would have been spared the flame. We know the earth is flat because the ships did not return. Clearly, many fell off the edge. My children see that there is no ice cream left. They think my husband ate it because he may have done so in the past. Actually it was me now, and it just might have been me in the past too.

If the monkey makes the connection between the track and the presence of the snake, he might choose to stay in the trees. If he is wrong, and there is no snake, what does he have to lose but an afternoon of play on a nice clear trail? I suppose we've evolved to make connections based, even, on slim evidence for the sake of self-preservation. It does lead to a lot of error, especially as our world has become more sophisticated and our perils more esoteric. How do we know if something is a clue or a product of our imagination or fear? To what extent should we avoid drawing connections? To what extent should we avoid assuming a causal relationship? Have we evolved now, to such a sophisticated state that we have the luxury of not making potentially specious connections? Is there any role for intuition or an evolved and embedded knowledge? Is the idea of tabula rasa, a clean slate, a pre-knowledge mind, just a fantasy?

Maybe the reason the monkey did not make the connection is a function of its condition as a high primate. Maybe our awareness of mistakes in evidence-based assumptions is also a selected trait in the Darwinian sense. Alternately, maybe the monkeys' choice of play says more about the selected need and value of play as it stacks up against the obvious goal of self-preservation. Perhaps play is essential to self preservation too, and the non-compromising of this, is representative of its importance to a species. Maybe play is a fear-crushing self-preservational tool. After all, creatures who live in fear do not prosper. They do not reproduce.

Are there conclusions? No. The monkey did not make the connection between the evidence and the danger, or the monkey made the connection and ignored it. If the former, it raises questions about their ability to make connections. If the latter, it might raise questions about what conditions are necessary for the advancement of a species. How important is play? Do we need play in order to be healthy; to heal?

What sort of play is possible in a healthcare experience? Is there a way to bring play into doctor's offices, treatments and testing? What does play look like in such a scenario?

If we look at the Colobus' behaviour that could be said to exhibit risk taking, we might ask ourselves what is tolerable risk? When confronted with the choice between, safety or fun, certainty or novelty, which should we choose?

In a scientific setting is innovation our version of play? How essential is innovation? If we don't innovate do we decay? Do we hesitate to accept new thinking in the world of healthcare because we find it threatening? What are we afraid of? How bad is a mistake? How big is that snake?

Buzz and Our Hunger for Society

The Health Strategy Innovation Cell founded the *Global Accelerator Award*. It's an award for creating buzz and chatter on the Web. Why is there an award for chatter? Didn't we get in trouble for this at school? What's the value of buzz? I wondered. I didn't get it.

A giant lever began to squeak in my mind. I could tell there was a great and powerful idea attempting to bust the rust on my gears. A great force was pulling against my pompous individualty. Steel scraped against steel as that giant idea pushed down on the lever of my stiff grey matter. It went down a quarter way, a half, and then three quarters. The gears lurched and clanged. Finally, as if with the assistance of all the minds in the world who'd already thought the thought, the idea succeeded. My gears sprang into activity. It's about the whole! It's about the machine. No, it's not a machine. It's an organism. No. It's not an organism. It is machine and organism combined. It's what happens when machine is used to connect organisms.

There's a great original Star Trek episode that features some "aliens" who don't have to communicate with words like we humans. The aliens have great big heads and on every Hallowe'en they have come to your house and stared at you without asking the old, "trick or treat" question. You, understanding, have stuffed their sacks with candy. These big-headed aliens really know how to talk without mouths. They get their messages across. Well, I think we humans, and more species, do communicate globally and even through time without words, but I don't think we understand this very well. In fact, I think it's downright ignored, maybe even denied by most of us. So, we need a bunch of translator tools which bring us together in a way we find manageable; like a language broadcaster. Am I talking about radio, phone or TV? No.

Twitter™? The term sounds like something unimportant. It sounds frivolous. To fritter away the afternoon, I twitter. It just doesn't seem to carry any significant bearing.

Who made up this word? I've been watching fritter from afar. I've been trying to understand the Twitter appeal. I've been watching people I really like and respect living all-a-Twitter, and I've been trying to determine what it is that I don't get about it.

There has been nastiness in the old-school newspaper about how it is a tool of the narcissist. There has been the suggestion that people just want to have a platform for their view. People just want to be published, it is said. They want something out in the world for posterity, I've been told. They want to be acknowledged. They are preachers without a platform, and bully bumper stickers without a bumper. Somehow that just didn't seem like the all of it to me or even the beginning. It is after all only a 140 character bleep.

I've heard of people using Twitter at innovation conventions. They tweet and Twitter a certain address and discover who else is attending. This seems like fun. They Twitter where they are going to be, and propose meeting up. "..@rbroom @genetics sympo lactose intolerance markers ..."

There is a tweet language and a tweet illiteracy.

"@bdnow tinyurl#..."

They even engage in the more prosaic messages.

"@rdnow join us@Donkey and Pickle 7," they tweet.

"Oh, OK," I say to myself. "It's kind of like a modern-day walkie-talkie."

But, nope. That use may be a part of the Twitter phenomenon but it is clear to me, that it isn't the all of it either. I stand back. What is it, I wonder? The Twitterers go on without me. Should I just get a Twitter account and find out? But I don't want to. I can't stand jumping onto this sort of bandwagon. Can't a person just live unconnected? Twitter is all facilitated by the World Wide Web, I understand. There's just so much bursting-out togetherness. Why is it good? Is it? According to many, it is.

The World Wide Web and Twitter are just the kind of tools we can use to get together. In fact, I think some version of them might lead to a world in which we operate as a large organism in a way that we're capable and willing to acknowledge. That's what Twitter channels do. They create organisms of instant thought. The message is different from a text, or an email or a phone call. They're like sound bites, but they are thought bites. They are little bursts of electricity from our brains. There's a real modesty in that and there is play. It's not narcissism. It's about being a part of and giving to a thought process larger than our own. It is playful and we learn from play. It's not perfect in functionality but the potential for creating a big common brain is there. Maybe that's why some celebrities like Twitter. They can participate in something beyond themselves. It's not so much about expanding their stellar orbit as it is bringing their identities into reality. Maybe it brings them into balance.

There's something called Trendsmap™ that's a bit like Google Earth™. A person who wants to know what people are interested in can use it as a tool. Type in a topic or place and the Twitter conversations will show up on the world map. It's amazing. You can see what is being chatted about in Lisbon right now. You can see how and where in the world people are thinking little bites of scary thought about lightning for example. At the time I'm writing there's a lot of chat about actresses who wear certain dresses, sports teams and a few flashy politicians.

The Global Accelerator Award is about the value of buzz. The buzz that is being celebrated circles around an idea or program that gets people thinking and communicating on issues affecting our health in a panoramic sense. It's the buzz that creates organisms of thought that grow and become effective.

The award celebrates an idea that hooks into the imaginations of a world of people who are all interested, invested and intellectually charged enough to create an organism based on the idea. It's a buzz that allows for others to participate in the refining and expanding of ideas and helping these notions step over the divide, into practice.

Buzz is active. It's instant. It's pulsing. It's pulsing like any single cell organism that is alive with the basic stuff of life: electricity. Bzzzz. Chatter. Bzzzz.

Just before Frankenstein came alive there was the great voice of the electric charge, and that voice of life said, " bzzzzzzzzzzzzzzzz"......

Ok, Frankenstein was a sad story and it was sad because the created individual had no community. The poor monster was lonely. Social media goes beyond the one-way use of the web. The electrified individual gets to link up in a world known as 3.0, and what happens there, happens in the musical Hair. This was celebrated in a different low tech reformative time, but the language is curiously the same.

"What's the buzz. Tell me what's a happenin?" - Hair, The Musical

The Gap Between the Ideal and the Real

Barbara W. Tuchman wrote in *A Distant Mirror*: "When the gap between the ideal and the real becomes too wide, the system breaks down. ....[and] "man retains his vision of order and resumes his search".

I just happened to put this book down at Chapter 7, for a little pause from the disembowelments and beheadings of the 14th Century, and picked up the book that I'd thrown into my bag. Attracted to it by healthcare considerations and the way we as physical beings negotiate our world. Knowing almost nothing about the famous author, I opened the book.

Experience and Nature by John Dewey seems to address this notion of the gap between the ideal and the natural. He seems to be suggesting that communication closes that gap and creates a sophistication of worldview that is special to human beings. We use the tools of communication, adapt the tools, and then end up in a new place.

Dewey points out that awareness of a space between the ideal and our real world is representative of consciousness, and this consciousness keeps us bright and switched on. Well Tuchman is saying that understanding things are not perfect keep us pushing forward and seeking better.

In Tuchman's subject, the 14th century, among other things, misery, treachery, lechery, thievery were part of the human process of pushing forward. That was gruesome. More esoterically, Dewey seems to posit that the awareness of an ideal, and the gap between it and our condition, is a manifestation of our consciousness, maybe even the starting point of our morality. He writes that art is the highest form of communicating the rift or repairing the 'gap'.

He laments the gap between art and science and seems to be calling for a romantic science. This is a science where human emotion and creativity inform the method, and I wonder if he would allow that madness and method come together in the best expression of science. Maybe he was referring to creativity and discovery.

A more holistic coming together of fundamental human qualities of emotion and reason, might inform our healthcare experience. Typically, in a healthcare experience there is a subversion of the patient's whole self. The patient becomes only a clinical specimen and the situation seems to create a problematic and pining result. The patient wants the experience to include her whole self. The patient profoundly feels the gap between the clinical reality, a splintered self, and the clinical ideal of a whole self. The patient comes away from the healthcare experience feeling diminished and maybe even rendered like a 14th century citizen. OK, not like a 14th century citizen who might then trip on her entrails.

Dewey seems to be suggesting that "the traditional separation of nature and experience" needs to be replaced with an idea of continuity. What does he mean by that? What could that mean within the context of our healthcare model? If we allow that there is a continuity that is the communication of our physical and mental selves maybe we can aspire toward a better healthcare experience. This is necessary on two levels. The first is in the very private meld of our mental and physical elements, and the second, is the communication between us and our healthcare professionals. I think we understand something profound is missing in the way we relate in the clinical setting, and I think that is one reason people are looking for a better healthcare experience.

As Tuchman said, we continue to try to close the gap. Dewey wrote that we do have the ability to communicate what he refers to as a naturalistic link. Let's do it. The healthcare relationships of our future could be amazing.

PARTICULAR

The Heidi Assumption

The turtles don't seem to mind that I'm sharing the rock with them here at the top of the French River in Ontario, Canada. Clearly I'm still enough so as not to disturb them, dumbstruck as I am, here in the reptile warming sun.

I guess I know how they feel covered over with a carapace. I've recognized in my thinking some assumptions, and what are assumptions if not a desensitizing exoskeleton?

I've just read Richard B. Wright's, *October*. I enjoyed it for many reasons including being carried along on a compelling journey. He created a world into which I could lend my imagination and gather full sounds and smells. He presented social and moral questions of a universal nature. He placed these questions on a platform of a timely concern; cancer, its prevalence, and what it might mean to look straight into a fatal diagnosis. He also, in a somewhat unimportant descriptive phrase revealed to me how easy it is to live for years in a state of unexplored ignorance, assuming knowledge and blind to my own arrogance even on a little matter.

It unfolded like this. Mr. Wright's character was making reference to Switzerland and his own limited knowledge of it. The character points to the two colourful and seemingly trite things that he associated with the country: cuckoo clocks and Heidi. Oh yes, I nodded as I read. I know cuckoo clocks and Heidi.

I remembered the day in the late 1960's when my Dad arrived home with a cuckoo clock. On every hour the miraculous counting bird appeared. Then, when the feathered mathematician was done showing off, a group of dancers trotted out onto the platform below him. In lederhosen and big skirts they danced around most expertly and lightly.

I could never understand why, as much as we kids tried to keep the pine cone chains that wound the thing charged, it inevitably shut down for hours on end. The pine cones would be drawn up high, way beyond the reach of small children even when standing on chairs or on each others' shoulders. The thing must have been torture for my Mum, and I think she tried to allay her suffering by tucking those pine cone drawstrings up under the bird's cherry wooded nether zone. The thing became permanently "broken" the day after my brother fell off my shoulders and split his forehead open on the baseboard. That's a cuckoo clock. It involves stitches.

"Cuckoo. Cuckoo."

Heidi. Oh yes, Heidi was the blond girl in braids who had some association with mountains with snowcaps and white aprons. She also lived in a sort of thatched roof dwelling. Wasn't there an old man involved? This was what I thought I knew of Heidi. I nodded and mentally checked off the reference as I read Mr. Wright's book. I sort of smiled to myself. Sure, I know what your character is saying. I read on. Then the rhythm of the story started to hit stop signs in my brain. My mental car sputtered. Who's Heidi? It sputtered and smoked.

"Jane, you've never read *Heidi*," squawked a voice, my integrity traffic cop.

My mental car clanked and stopped.

"Jane, even if it's just a light reference by the author, and not intended to stop the story, you have no idea what *Heidi* is all about," reprimanded the voice.

"She yodels," I hollered!

"You're just a poseur," said the cop, writing me up.

"I'm not going to read stupid *Heidi*," I responded indignantly, silently and with contempt.

"Yes, that's exactly what you're going to do.'"

So, I swore a bit and realized that I better do just that. Here I sit with the turtles, hot on the rock on the French. From the library of a cabin I have pulled off a 1913 edition of, yes, *Heidi*. You see, this area, and other north lake country like it in Canada, was rather popular among the Canadians of early vintage. They came to these wet wooded places with books, and thick pressed glass and their crated Limoges. They brought bagpipers, Molson ale, dinner dress and leather bound gold embossed *Heidi* by Johanna Spyri.

I'm sitting here with the turtles and I'm hyperglycemic as black-haired Heidi is rushing through my veins sticky and sweet. I'm on page two hundred and eighty-three and the girl is just so happy and not ruined by feather hats as her grandfather might say. I think I'm all for a little ruination as I begin to topple over, dizzy, with the beauty of the sunset over the Alps and the good hearts of the bouncing goats. I'm getting the blurry picture as my blood pressure returns to a normal range. I'm beginning to know what *Heidi* is about. I reach for a glass of bitter lemonade. I'll have to read on. The temptation to put the book down is pretty high, but then I might continue to assume that I know *Heidi*. Would I have the courage to say I don't know? I look at the turtles and wonder. I'm not so sure given my chequered history. I better resolve this problem of myself as a fake, at least, on all matters *Heidi*.

How many unimportant things do we just assume? Onto how many important matters do we layer assumptions without consciousness of having done so? Apologies, Richard B Wright, *October* is worth a much wider consideration, but this just happened to be a part of my experience of it. The insidiousness of assumption surely covers heavy over our thinking like the shell over a real slow tortoise.

...back to *Heidi*. The turtles stretch their necks and look at me with eyebrows raised.

The "Of Course" Factor

"Of course".

This expression comes with a few meanings, but the one I'm interested in is the one that has a revelatory smell.

Does, "of course" mean something is on course? Does it mean something is expected? On the contrary, what is missing in the written version of the expression is the accompanying surprise, or "aha" that bursts from the speaker. There is maybe a smile or a slapping of the knee. There is often an implied, "Why didn't I think of that?"

Personally, when I've had the urge to respond, "Of course", I'm reacting to something that is reasonable but fresh. The "of course' object will have opened my eyes. It is, maybe, of a natural progression, but some thing or act or notion that points in a direction I'd never considered. I wonder how I could not have seen this most obvious thing, "How could I not have considered this," I ask myself?

"Is it possible I once did not know this," I shake my head and wonder?

I've had this experience with the simplest things. I discovered this recently as I made a purchase of a package of sewing needles. The package looked the same as it has for years and years but the device itself had changed. At first I didn't notice the redesign. The package came with instructions and I scoffed tossing it aside. Are they kidding? Who needs instructions to thread a needle? I loathe instructions. Then it occurred to me that something might be up. It was. I glanced at the package. The sewing needle had been redesigned. It had a slit ridge in the top for easy threading. Of course this seemed positively rudimentary, yet since the sewing of skins we've all been squinting to thread the whale bone. Now, all a person need do is pass the thread across the top of the little steel device and give it a tug.

"Voila."

The needle is threaded. Will a camel now pass more easily?

Poets often fall into the "aha" category of performer. Suddenly someone tries coupling words or sounds in a way that has yet to be brought forth in literary circles and it seems it was a genre that always was. Comedians live on the "aha" moment . Ordinary things suddenly take on the obviously ridiculous like, olive oil, almond oil, canola oil...baby oil.

Does all innovation come out of incremental steps? Will the most profound healthcare innovation be a simple, eye-opening, "of course" affair? It is probably so, and it may come from the most unexpected mind through an unexpected medium. We will collectively slap our hopefully healthy patellae and rejoice?

Ah...but, of course!"

Cancer: Our Collective Autobiography

I'm still reading *A Distant Mirror: The Calamitous 14th Century*, by Barbara W. Tuchman which was published in 1978. It's funny how it's shaping my thoughts today. There is much that's interesting about it. Ms. Tuchman was very clear about her purpose in writing the book. She declares her intentions in the very first line.

"The genesis of this book was a desire to find out what were the effects on society of the most lethal disaster of recorded history – that is to say The Black Death of 1348-50, which killed an estimated one third of the population living between India and Iceland."

The woman is really clear about her subject. The next thing that struck me as lucid is her method.

"I have chosen a particular person's life as the vehicle of my narrative. Apart from human interest, this has the advantage of enforced adherence to reality."

She goes on to explain this in more detail and it caused me to pause and think over her choice. I have to agree with the idea of biography, or a biographical approach, as illuminating if written in a way that encompasses the world around the subject and articulates the nuances well. What Ms. Tuchman did, with *A Distant Mirror* was to choose a person of distinction, but was for her purposes, mid-line. She chose what we might dub a representative citizen: a squire. Through this technique, she expected to be able to reveal the fine points of the age.

This idea invited me to reflect about self. It's not so much that I was thinking about "I", I was thinking, rather, about "We". Who are we?

I think the most ordinary person of our age is either the cancer patient or the surviving loved one. I'm not sure which. I think a dichotomous narrative of time lived, post-diagnosis, would be incredibly revealing about the concerns of our day to day lives, our values and our larger society. Surely there must be other good examples of the ordinary person of our age: a high school student or a teacher, a white collar middle manager, a builder, a retail worker, an active environmentalist.

On the other hand, few high school students have much in common with builders and the middle manager and teacher live very differently in the typical weekday hour. An alternative common person might be the environmentalist, because after all, each of us live on this earth and will prosper or suffer under the follies of our consumptive habits. However, people debate this subject. So, the best example of our commonality is our humble physical selves. We all have bodies. We all can get sick. On the top of the charts, on the hit list of maladies, is cancer.

So the question now, is what can we learn about ourselves by reading the biography of our most common citizen? There are some historian's pitfalls of which we should be conscious. Ms. Tuchman writes, "A greater hazard built into the very nature of recorded history, is overload of the negative: the disproportionate survival of the bad side − of evil, misery, contention and harm."

Ok, so in looking at the lives of our most representative citizens let's be careful to try to look at them completely. The sheer suffering and sorrow will be the easiest thing to see. Let's look at other aspects of these lives that are common to us.

Hmm. Ok I'll go first. I don't have cancer. My immediate family members are, so far as we know, cancer free. I've lost a number of aunts and uncles and friends to cancer. There is something, I can say they all shared, besides the misery and the suffering. They were all incredibly noble as their lives ended and they showcased this nobility through a prism of bright wit. They were kind about their healthcare workers and they were hilarious about the indignities of their failing bodies. They just didn't complain. Sometimes they got a little feisty, but that was the spirit in them. So far, that's my biggest take-away in terms of their commonality. That's incredibly positive, don't you think? The other biggest commonality is that they left people behind who were not ready for their deaths, who felt surprised, shocked and ripped apart by the loss of their love.

The commonality in the cancer world, of course, is healthcare. What is the experience like for the patient and the families? Do they receive the kind of treatment that they think is appropriate, even if they could not be saved? Is there a satisfaction that our society's healthcare promise is upheld? Either way, what does it say about our humanity? What does it say about our times? What is our healthcare promise?

Of the 14th Century, Ms. Tuchman is writing about a time much different from ours, but she maintains that certain historical truths hold. When there is a gap between the society's principles and everyday life, a problem arises that demands to be addressed. Of those times, she talks about the institutions of order: the church, the king, the ranks of chivalry. She points to the ruling classes as really messing things up. Who are the ruling classes of our world, and more specifically of our healthcare world? Is there a gap between our principles and our experience?

The historian writes: "When the gap between the ideal and the real becomes too wide, the system breaks down. ....[and] "man retains his vision of order and resumes his search".

The search for the ideal continues. The search in Tuchman's terms downloaded into some real corruption and brutality like the bloody dismantling of fiefdoms, the gouging of various eyeballs and the bartering of immortality by the leaders of the church. That's pretty serious. Well, I'm glad things aren't this bleak. In fact, we live in a more collaborative age where there are no obvious evil squires and our expectations of collaboration are high and usually fulfilled. We live in an age where high expectations of personal and environmental health are reasonable. We have, however, seen a dark side. We do recognize that something is amiss. We are not healthy. Among other ailments, we are all getting cancer; a strange phenomenon of cell over-production. Now that's metamorphic for our times! Outside of the necessary environmental questions about cause, what do the commonalities of the healthcare experience and our dying tell us?

There must be something we can learn from our collective autobiography. Perhaps we could begin a conversation that attempts to come to the core of what is common in our cancer experience, and in so doing, gain a better understanding of our age, our character, and of any gaps between our principles and our reality. Who knows, maybe in writing our collective autobiography we will reveal something that until now, has been hidden from ourselves.

Refresh the Ipod. Refresh Ideas

It's one of those warm late afternoons in an Ontario June and I've just arrived home from a run. I feel invigorated, partly because I threw in a few hills to up the ante. I really enjoy running in the ravine that snakes through the watershed valley. The trees grow over the path and it has a hobbit trail feel to it. I run happy.

After my first child was born I stayed by his side for a long time. It was important to me that he knew I would always be right there for him. I just couldn't stand the idea that he might cry and that I wouldn't come. For months we were glued together. Then one sunny June day my husband returned from work early.

"Why don't you go for a run?"

"I wonder. Do you think I could?" I asked, looking out longingly at the world that lay beyond our front porch.

"Of course, he'll be fine."

I said nothing but went upstairs and changed into the running clothes that I had not worn for an incredibly long period of time. I came down and put on my shoes. My husband held the baby. I stepped out onto the porch and on the steps tied my laces. I lingered about the front garden, pulled a weed and watered a plant or two.

"Just go."

So, I turned and began to walk away from the house. My baby called out. I broke into my beginning trot. He began to cry. I looked back and my husband encouraged me with a shooing hand. I went back to the baby and rubbed my face on his. I turned and ran. I picked up speed. I could hear my baby crying. Friends, in our cheek by jowl neighbourhood, encouraged me onward.

"He's OK. He'll be fine. Go"

I turned back. "No, really go," they said.

I ran back toward home, just so I could see my husband and child and they seemed to be working it out. I turned again, my neighbours shooed me with their hands, and I ran like wild game. I had never felt so light. There was such a spring in my legs. I felt weightless, truly weightless. In a minute I was at the entrance to the ravine. As I descended, the damp cool air filled my lungs and the city sounds filtered through the leaves and trickling water. The early bright green of the new summer filled my eyes and my legs flew. A liberating joy filled me, and if ever there was a bird lighter than this postpartum mother, I'd like to have known her. I was the very spirit of flight.

That was a lot of years ago. We moved away and moved again and again. We've lived in all sorts of different places and then this past year we've come back. Here we are in the same neighbourhood in which I walked my babies in the double stroller and had to make return trips to various stores as my pre-toddlers loved to pull things from shelves and smuggle them out. They were involved in various heists including the pilfering of shoe store foot sizers, loaves of bread, and flashlights. Anything they could sneak into the stroller was game. The reason they liked it so much is because of my reaction. On discovery of the hot item, I couldn't help but laugh and admonish and laugh. They'd convulse with laughter as they'd duped me again. A two year old and a three year old are, in conspiracy, unbelievably successful mother teasers. We'd arrive home. I'd lift them out of the stroller and one little hand would reach in to show me the loot, or I'd find it lodged underneath, having left a mirrored impression on a pudgy leg. Me laughing and they baby-dancing in delight, I'd load them back into the double stroller and we'd head back to the stores to confess our crimes.

So now when I run in the ravine that time period washes over me. It's great to be home. Today, I was thinking about the songs on my ipod. I ran and skipped from one song to the next. Some of these songs I would have listened to again and again last year, and would have happily jogged with them. Some, I now have absolutely no interest in hearing. What determines which ones will continue in my aesthetic and which ones will not? There are some that I've transferred or re-recorded from device to every modernizing device. I had a Rolling Stones period as I ran around the Central Park reservoir and from my west side address to an east side destination. Then came Verdi and Montserrat Caballe. *Pace, Mio Dio* got me through the mid-section of the run and past the hippos of Brooklyn's Prospect Park zoo.

Rittorna Vincitor always came just when needed, as I went up and down stone steps in the foggy grays of an early Venetian morning. Climbing a steep slope in Port Hope, Ontario I'd either focus intently on Schumann's *Frauenliebe und Leben* that I was trying to learn, or I'd laugh my legs into motion with Johnny Cash's, *Ring of Fire*. Running in South Carolina I found my ipod loaded with toothless old timer recordings that I'd picked up at the local establishment, Bill's Pickin' *Parlor*. The old fellers sat gumless with their banjos strummin' and tappin and knockin down tracks for posterity and strangers to enjoy. Today's hill buster is *Boom Boom Pow* or the knee lifter *Jagged Little Pill*, now, a classic.

Some music from these times gone by I'll still run with. Some I'll discard. What determines the changing aesthetic? Why does some music, although, I've heard it many times still appeal to me? Does an evolving aesthetic affect ideas as well? Do we hang on to some ideas simply because we came to them at certain rich times of life? Do we cling to ideas because they happened upon us, or we them, during a period of exceptional significance? How many decisions in government policy, that affect us profoundly, still hold simply because they were established during ideological and historically rich periods? How do we recognize these for what they are, not valuable in themselves but only relevant to us, as a society, in context and therefore possibly stale or in need of evaluation? Songs and policies are a bit the same. Sometimes things just get dated and that's because we've grown. We've found new ways of thinking, or we've evolved through experience, and have engaged in a kind of taste-testing that has developed new opinion forming receptors. We might want to consider this. I know for sure, it's time for me to refresh my ipod.

Meow

I've got the noisiest cat in the world. My husband every now and then thinks we should take her to a vet for ultrasound, blood work and maybe a barium enema.

"OK, take her." I say, with a sort of 'holy cow' in my tone.

He's concerned for the creature. He's kind. I'm not that kind about her. She drives me crazy. Ok, I like her too, but she's seriously high maintenance. She's always been noisy. She's been noisy since the day we adopted her. She was vicious then too. If the boys, just toddlers at the time, caught her at the wrong moment she'd slash with sharpened claws. What were we doing with this dangerous creature?

We'd just moved into an old farmhouse owned by the school where my husband worked. The place was entirely enchanting and as porous as can be. There were small animals who scurried secretly. Large animals walked openly as though on a libertine ark. In the spring the groundhogs came up the basement stairs and knocked at the door.

The first time I heard the knock on the door, I was a little cautious. What if it's a skunk? I'd smelled a lot of skunks. Our whole house even got skunked once. It was so bad that a woman stood beside me at a store holding her nose with a tissue. I stepped toward her. She stepped away. I inched toward her. She inched away. It wasn't a skunk that knocked though. It was a baby groundhog followed by a line-up of brothers, sisters, and cousins.

I opened the door and the little team captain hissed and snapped his teeth in a threatening babyish gesture. I closed the door, and thought this over. It seemed the gang wanted out of the basement and they had moved toward the light. It was morning and at that time of day, the sun shone at the back of the house, not at the front where their entrance was. I guess the sun coming from under the basement door and down the stairs was the beacon. Close to the basement door was the back door of the house which led onto a charming old style open porch. There, on warm days, I fed my boys and it was there that they did their artwork. So I opened the back door and created a sort of livestock trough with the backs of laundry baskets and whatever else was available. I didn't particularly want them scurrying about the house and going the way of the rabbit that died under the bookcase. When I'd completed construction of the exit route, I opened the basement door again. The whole demanding party of baby groundhogs marched out the basement. They hissed and slipped on the wooden floor and scuffed the varnish as they sought traction and as I shepherded them out. They asked and got what they wanted. It became a morning routine and I never denied them. They grew fat and happy.

So our adopted cat, who also doesn't hesitate to ask to have her needs fulfilled, enjoyed the house and was instantly mouse effective. The morning after her arrival at the farmhouse we awoke on a battlefield. The corpses of mice were strewn here and there. I found guts smeared across the dining room floor. Her prized victims, the Hectors, and all Khans and sons of mouse kings were laid out on the floor beside our beds. She left a gift for each of us for three days.

We learned to look before putting our feet down. One misstep was all it took to get that hard-wired. Then the gifts ceased. The mice were gone. They'd left the house. The cat pranced. Then when the winter came, no matter how cold, she took to sleeping in the groundhog lair with the hibernating gestating mother groundhogs. I know what you're thinking, yes, that cat was a vermin transporter.

Now, our retired sanitized urban cat meows for food, for water, to come in or to go out. She meows if you pass by where she rests. She meows to say hello and she meows to say goodbye. She meows to let me know that it's 4:45 am. She meows to tell me that she is in the tree. She meows to get attention and to get exactly what she wants. She almost always gets it.

Is there a lesson in this? Should I meow this much? Should we all ask for what we want with this sort of persistence? Is she just communicating? Is there something good to be found in persistently nudging others? Don't we just make a nuisance of ourselves? Are innovative people concerned with being a nuisance? Facebook offers a prompt to "poke Bill". Didn't that used to be a needling, teasing sort of action? In old fashioned Grade 1 public school that's all that was required to get the dunce cap and the stool in the corner. Does my ever prompting asking cat understand that nothing comes, no rubicon is crossed, no full bowl guaranteed, and no idea is hatched without a certain poking intrusive meow?

The Agile Blue Varmints

The teams, the Blues Varmints and the Bumble Bees, look at each other under brows streaked in mud. Uniforms sport great thick glops of wet earth. Parents stand on the sideline under rain coats and giant umbrellas. The coaches and the refs teach the boys, even, as the game is played. The spirit is nurturing and upbeat.

The blue team is made up of small players. The little Blues are fast and gritty tough. They give all their opponents a surprising and full game. They are even beginning to win most games. The yellow and black team is huge, and with the horizontal stripes on their uniforms, they look like over-satiated bumble bees. Their socks fall and the yellow stripes are darkened with mud. They are formidable. This team of Bumble Bees gains possession of the ball, and steadily moves it up the field. The drone with the ball slows and looks around, turning his body with the urgency of a Buddha shifting on a pillow.

"Bzzzz. Bzzzz z"

The Blue rushes and attempts to tackle. The great Bumble Bee continues to press forward. Little Blue Varmints swarm and try to bring the Bumble down. After immense effort...bzzzzt...they succeed. The Blue Varmints spring up in celebration as the ball is now in their possession. The kindly Bumbles do not emote but slowly walk to the end of the field. The Blues vibrate with enthusiasm and they communicate strategy and encouragement. They decide to pass. They plan to pass slippery and fast. Down on the other end of the mud puddle field, the Bumbles Bees look down and study their unlaced shoes.

Just an hour previously the Blues had played an entirely different kind of team. That team wasn't big. They were fast. The Blues had to speed up. They began passing like they never had before. They tackled lower and dove for their opponents. They won the game. What seems to work for the Blues is their ability to change. They are agile. They reinvent their game to meet the challenges of their opponents. They remain happy. They deny mild injuries and they keep moving. The Blue Varmints win the games and the steady Bumble Bees hold a solid second in the tournament.

They are all little boys playing rugby on a Saturday morning in the rain; some agile, some steady. One team innovates. The other presses on.

Silence, Space and Nothingness

Just thinking....spoke with a man tonight who is an ordained priest of the Anglican Church. He came into his collar after a career in business at the international CEO level. One human problem that has carried over from his corporate life to his ministerial work is the dilemma of addiction.

He used to see it in the employees at his companies. He would call people in for a talk and help them create an action plan. We now call these engagements "interventions", but they weren't called anything when he began. He just said to the alcoholic employee, "Either you let me drive you to rehab tonight, or you're fired."

It was a pretty simple action plan. The now Priest said this was usually preceded by months of phone calls from distraught spouses berating him for ruining their loved ones with overwork. That certainly sounds like the workforce of a bygone era. Any spouse today would assume that such a call would end not only the corporate association, but the marriage too. Not so then. After he assured the spouse he would look into the matter, and then confirming the problem, he, as the man of authority, presented the cold ultimatum to the employee.

"They knew I could either save their job or fire them, and this proved very effective."

Today the Priest says he continues counseling people on addiction problems. Now, the problem is drugs as well. He continues to speak to families. He may not be able to fire people from their work anymore, but his particular road map to a suggested eternity gives him influence. As well, people are simply drawn to the man. They find him helpful.

He told me, these days, organizations with big addiction problems are law firms. Lawyers are disproportionately addicted to all sorts of uppers. The legal firms put immense pressure on young lawyers to produce and they find themselves working longer and longer hours. They cope, with drugs.

"They buy into the firm's rewards system. It's not as though they are unwilling participants. I've counseled many."

Doctors, too, are known for drug abuse. Clearly, they have access to drugs but they also have the instituted phenomenon of extended work periods and sleep deprivation. If medical residents were given more sleep would drug abuse decline among these groups?

I was once at a dinner party where a guy introduced himself in a manner that was rather revved up. He volunteered that he was a brain surgeon. He seemed as though he had a scalpel and saw in his pocket at the ready. I clutched my head, pretending to smooth my hair. Luckily, Dr. Eager knew the hostess wouldn't want her carpet bloodied. Thank goodness she was so finicky.

He was surely on a fast moving train on which there was no room for thinking, subtlety or change. This seemed a little disturbing in a brain surgeon. Was he high? Yes Ma'am in one way or another, I'd say.

Maybe it's time to evaluate parameters of success. Skilled performance and even innovation might come with slowing down. This seems to be accepted in the world of art where it is widely documented.. Do other kinds of innovation require silence, space and nothingness too? Why wouldn't they?

Rules are Made to be Broken

My children are outside. They've braided together all of the elastics found in the house and they've made a sling shot. One is standing in the middle of the street swinging it and trying to achieve consistency in the toss. A rock the size of a lime is looped through the pouch he's crafted. The other advises on technique and style.

Whoosh. Whoosh. Whoosh.

He swings it again and again. He's getting faster and more accurate of aim. A couple walks by with a baby and a toddler. My boys pause. They look at each other.

"Don't hit the baby," one says to the other.

Then they laugh like the nine and eleven years olds that they are. These nine and eleven year olds are not that big on babies. Babies are somehow an insult to them. In a way that is not serious they imagine hitting the baby. It's all a bit of a cartoon in their minds. They look down at the ground feeling bad they've had the thought. They look down to the ground as if already in trouble and imagining the crying child.
The boys stand still. The couple and the children pass by.

Whoosh. Whoosh. Whoosh.

They love to create things. They like to have pals come over and dismantle everything electric and rebuild it all into something new. They attach wheels to lawn chairs and ride them crazily down the nearest hill.

"Mum, we've made some really good ammo and it's going to go a hundred yards," one reports enthusiastically.

"Wow," I respond.

We have ongoing talks about safety. I insist on protective goggles.

I talk about their eyes and other people's eyes. Helmets hang at the ready. Then plans change and they are off on their bikes. We talk about the dangers of going onto the train tracks.

"Don't do it. Someone was killed just a few months ago," I warn.

"Don't go into the ravine, there are creeps down there."

"Where's the ravine, Mum?"
I slap my cranium. I've created a curiosity by the very mention of it.

They are in the workroom now. I hear the snip of the pointy-nosed pliers as they cut through wire. Something new is being rigged up. It thrills me. I love that they want to create things, build things and invent things. I like that they want to explore.

"Mum, we need to drill a hole."

I become party to the invention and provide drilling service.

"Stop. Let's see," they instruct.
I stop. They look at the tube into which I'm drilling a big hole.

"You need to bring it this way."

The oldest grabs a pencil and draws a line for me to target. The younger inspects his brother's design. They agree. They pass me the tube and I engage the drill.

"Stop," they instruct. "Perfect."

It fills me with hope that their lives will be plump with happiness, as the simple pleasures of creation are visceral to them. I think they'll find happy occupations and purpose in that. They'll have bright colleagues with exciting ideas with whom they'll work hard, take a break and eat sandwiches under trees. So, I have to help them keep themselves safe (snip) as they (snip) explore this world. I have to make sure I don't stifle their enthusiasm with warnings. I need to protect them from any societal chastisement that comes from breaking silly rules. I want them to break lots of rules. No, more accurately, I want them to be conscious.

I know that they are kind and good fellows, so I know they won't hurt others or commit petty crimes. I know that most of the rules they break will be foolish rules that only limit and stifle. There'll be some missteps and some rules that shouldn't have been broken, maybe. Then they'll know what ones are valid. snip. ...smash snip...

They're making a blow gun, together. Their cousin has arrived at the door. We'll get another pair of safety goggles. The excitement is fantastic.

Innovation hangs in the air around them like moisture before the biggest thunderstorm of all time.

INSTITUTIONAL

Courting Risk, Sharpening the Mind

This morning in a conversation with Lorna Jean Edmonds, Assistant Vice-President International Relations of the University of Toronto, Lorna Jean raised the idea of "risk" as a positive. I listened. In her work with the University of Toronto she has seen risk translate into a catalyst for innovation. As a person with an active international mind, a mind of a traveller, I wondered if Lorna Jean was also thinking about risk as it is presented by Eric J. Leed in his 1991, *The Mind of the Traveller: From Gilgamesh to Global Tourism*. Dr. Leed begins his examination of the mind of the traveller with the very roots of the word in Indo-European languages. (pg5) "where travel and experience are intimately wedded terms.

The Indo-European root of experience is *per*. [...] *Per* has been construed as "to try," "to test," "to risk" connotations that persist in the English word peril. [...] "Many of the secondary meanings of *per* refer explicitly to motion "to cross space," "to reach a goal," "to go out". The connotation of risk and danger implicit in peril are also obvious in the Gothic cognates for *per* in which *p* becomes an *f* fern (far), fare, fear, ferry. "

The author elaborates further on the connection of risk, fear, travel and resultant wisdom which, in the old German, was found in the adjective "bewandert" which meant "well travelled" as a virtue. This suggests a long held belief of value inherent in travel, and suggests through exposing ourselves to the unknown and facing peril we learn and become wiser.

This morning, Lorna Jean was talking about the effect on thinking when inventors or scientists see, first-hand, what is happening in their field internationally. When they visit a lab in a place away from home they will have heightened observational reflexes for this is part of the phenomenon of travel. They sometimes see that thinkers in different places have methods unlike their own. These differences are on display.

Otherness in method and analysis can illuminate assumptions and errors in their own work. Thinkers who discover flaws in their methods face the bleak reality that their professional world is at risk. Their day to day intellectual passions are threatened. Confronted with this, the courageous thinker accepts the challenge. Discovery of this risk is positive and transformative. It often catapults the thinker to the next level of discovery. LJ believes travel is a profound way to find risk, refine research, and expand thinking.

So who are the travellers of our world? There are so many: Darwin and Columbus, Champlain and Franklin, Marco Polo across Asia, Stark and Lawrence in the Middle East, the world powers to the moon.

The University of Toronto's great Mathematician Donald Coxeter is said to have become interested in geometry as he considered H.G. Wells' *The Time Machine*. He began to try to draw out a fourth dimension in shapes and forms in order to come up with a practical application of this most novel way of travel, time travel, and this formed in his mind the idea of hyper-dimensional geometries. Coxeter, as a boy boarded the train to Cambridge together with his nervous Dad, and went to visit Bertrand Russell who helped the family plan the boy's mathematical education. Later with the coming of WWII Coxeter accepted an invitation to join the faculty of the University of Toronto. Imagine the concern when facing a life in this the coldest of colonies.

There is no question that risk was primary to all these journeys. There is also no question that risk faced head-on has expanded our world. We'd think that in self-preservation we humans would avoid risk, but we don't. I suppose as much as we've evolved to survive, we've also evolved to learn, to be curious and this sometimes translates into play. It seems we've evolved to play. Play can be risky. Ask any parent. Sometimes play is about adventure.

Risk is the very stuff of adventure, and courage is the stuff of risk. How has this translated culturally? We exalt the courageous. The courageous are the subjects of our favourite stories. We identify the courageous as our heroes, visionaries and leaders. So we inculcate in our children a hunger to be heroes and the heroes of current times are the innovators in art and science, business and sport. The inventors must push beyond their knowledge. Every innovator must seek to be a hero, an adventurer, a pioneer, courageous, fearless, peril seeking and a miner of the unknown.

I suppose there isn't much that sharpens the mind more than thinking you just might sail off the edge of the world, and sailing toward the precipice anyway. Risk sharpens the eye of the watchman in the crow's nest, and heightens all the senses of the crew. Courting risk, we sharpen our minds.

Age of Method – a supra-paradigm shift

Today, in conversation with Robert Phillips, Deputy Director of the Ontario Institute for Cancer Research, I was turned a few beautiful degrees in a new direction. I know I often get attached to a way of thinking, and then something comes along to blast me off my position. It's guaranteed that it'll come. Well, it always has and this brings me to remember a good opinion toppling tome, *The Drunkard's Walk* by Leonard Mlodinow. I'm trying to discipline myself to go back to this book over and again. It forces me to pause, and reveals to me shadows in my constructions.

Bob Phillips also showed me a shadow. I told him I wanted to talk about methods of collaboration. The Ontario Institute for Cancer Research is all about collaboration in scientific research. I've been wondering if we are returning to an age of collaboration. This is reminiscent of early society on which the very foundations were collaboration. We might look at Thomas Kuhn as collaboration and method apply to science.

With a twist, Thomas Kuhn's *Structure of Scientific Revolutions* might be relevant. To use the language of today, Kuhn presented the idea of paradigm as an order of metrics onto which theories and discoveries are tested and layered. In Kuhn's description it is when experimental results can no longer be grafted onto the paradigm, or metrics, that a shift begins to occur. It may take a few scientific results or questions which are incompatible with the paradigm before scientists concur that the paradigm needs to be recalibrated or shifted. In terms of scientific revolution Kuhn's famous phrase "paradigm shift" is referring to the science itself.

There has been another "paradigm shift", but the paradigm that has so dramatically shifted is not the pure science paradigm that is all about the metrics on which experimental results are calibrated, the shift has come in the very notion of that which is the primary paradigm of science, the method itself. Let's call it a supra-paradigm shift. An urgency to move from theory to lab table to treatment room just may have spawned this. The Ontario Institute for Cancer Research has been established to recreate the way scientists work together and to facilitate the sharing of systems and ideas. Ultimately, the mandate of the OICR is to move discovery from the "bench to the clinic". They want to improve cancer treatment, not just cancer knowledge. The OICR has done a number of things to meet this end. They've improved the efficiency of clinical trials through infrastructure. For any promising lead they've established one budget, one lawyer and one contract process with all involved players. They've created a single ethics approval panel. They've streamlined.

Is this change sufficient to speed results of the lab into the clinic? No. More was required. Dr. Phillips explains a phenomenon called, "the valley of death". The biggest stall from promising discovery to treatment is the midline point. It's the great divide that we humans meet across genres. I like to think of it as the ever -reappearing and demanding leap of faith - the leap over the big abyss of ignorance.

By the time potential is found along a line of discovery, a budget has already been spent. There is a next stage, where an investment must be made to delve into feasibility of mass production or treatment. This is another expensive stage. Investors have a hard time jumping in at this point, because, often, what looks promising does not pan out. Discovery let-down is fundamental to scientific research and all involved understand this. Enter the OICR. with a panel of analysts of various disciplines the Institute determines what research has the most potential of a pool of submitted proposals. "We asked, 'what do you have that looks promising?

Those selected were invited into a two stage funding process. An advisory panel established proscribed steps. Halfway through the first installment of funding the projects were reviewed. If all had gone according to plan, and if business interests were "sniffing" around the lab, another investment was approved. By the time this process was completed, the risk for a major investor was significantly decreased. In the four years since the founding of the OICR two projects have moved to the commercial or treatment side, and others are in process.

In addition to this attempted tackling of the "valley of death", the OICR has established the Ontario Tumor Bank. The goal is to provide samples of annotated tumors that can be used for research which refines treatment. They'd successfully banked about 625 by September 2009. The coordination among institutions to achieve this is a significant feat. It would seem to make sense, then, that the Institute might be able to help me understand this age of collaboration. I started with the basic question.

"Do you think that is how we would classify this age of science – an age of collaboration.?"

Bob Phillips looked skeptical.

"I haven't really thought about it." He rolled it over in his mind.

He then explained that one of the research challenges in this age of investigation is the sheer speed at which data come pouring at the scientists. Calculations and samplings, data of all kinds are so quickly available to the researcher that the labs have to be very methodical about handling the rush of findings. Sheer information pours at them. The labs need efficiency and remarkable skills of collation in order to remain investigative and not overwhelmed. They need systems and structure. The faster they can get to make sense of this data the faster the results will show promise. The faster cancer treatments will progress.

So what hit me smack on the noggin' is the realization that this is not just an age of collaboration, it truly is more an age of method. Sure collaboration is here for all kinds of reasons and this is part of the increase in speed of data, but method will reign as facts splash down in a torrent. It doesn't matter how many people are collaborating if all the results cannot be handled and understood. So, in the hindsight of the history of science, if we manage to succeed, while collaboration is a big part of these times and one reason for the new rate of data collection, the other being technological progress , we may ultimately declare this scientific period as The Age of Method.

Flux – Who's a Doctor?

We don't like reflux. That's stuff going backwards. Most of us want things to move along efficiently. Efflux, on the other hand, is usually super. Efflux is the success of a pump getting rid of toxic substances. Very nice. Reflux and efflux are both about motion. Anything in flux involves motion. Lots of things can be in motion like trains, water, romance, and even professions.

The medical profession is in flux. This living profession grows, evolves and hits plateaus, and then a social stimulus comes along. There is a bump. Medical practice moves and adapts. It has always done that. That's good to know. It keeps the profession seeking and its collective synapses firing. A key to the consideration of the status of the medical profession, though, seems to be the requirements of its particular form of flux. What are the variables on this moving vector?

For Euclid, in Physics and Engineering, flux is a vector and a vector is not only about moving in a certain direction. It's also concerned with what is required to achieve that movement. In the life sciences the notion of flux is often a quantifier. It might refer to rate of change or volume of change or the differential. Sometimes, *flux* refers to a catalyst. In the world of medicine it signifies many things. After all, there are lots of fluids, chemicals, magnetic and electrical signals in the human body to monitor, both in treatment and in the laboratory.

There is flux in the identity of a doctor. The title doctor as we now use it came from the latin *doctus* or wise man. The original doctus was a *doctor* of Arts of the Sorbonne of the 13th century. Who is a doctor? We use the term to refer to our physicians. What is the role of doctor? This has been a question since the beginning of human relationships, since the beginning of Homo Sapien Sapien and maybe before that. Is the chimpanzee who removes the lice from the sufferer, a good citizen, a friend, a hygienist, a caregiver, or maybe just a fellow who likes to tinker? If there is one chimpanzee among the group who is especially expert at achieving delousing results, does she become thought of as the expert? As she builds her skills and increases her prowess, do others come to her for treatment and alleviation of their suffering? Is she a doctor? Maybe she's a technician. If she has a great compassion for the sufferer and a desire to help, is she then a doctor? Are higher values plus high value skill essential to the designation of doctor? Maybe so and that's a Confucian definition.

The earliest peoples had doctors in the form of shamans and medicine men who were set apart from the group. Often these people were revered. Sometimes they were feared. They were thought to have mystical access and a special relationship with the deities of nature.

The identity of a doctor seems inseparable from an analysis of the doctor/patient relationship. After all, there is no doctor without a patient. The Ancient Greeks talked about the many different kinds of love and, from this, they formed ways of practicing medicine. The notion of correct practice of medicine became much discussed along with the proper degrees of love of self, which was inherently connected to a love of friends for whom sacrifice would be made, and it also included the love of the natural world. The assumption of the role of doctor was highly conscious, studied, regimented, and somewhat coolheaded.

During the Dark Ages in Europe, the classical practices of medicine were lost and all sorts of self-proclaimed healers took to up the knife, unguents and goo. There was a surge of lay doctors and curious healers living in shacks over the hills and above the pond. There was often no ongoing doctor patient relationship. The methods might have been gruesome, the suffering high, and occasionally the treatment was effective or declared effective.

As the Middle Ages settled in, the priests began to take on the role of the doctor. This was partly because they were almost the only people with any education. They were also considered to be close to God and therefore the best able to pray for a good outcome. Priests were known to carry on all sorts of treatments without the slightest bit of training and only the confidence of their prayers to support their actions. The doctor of the Middle Ages assumed responsibility not only for the physical health of the patient but also the eternal health. Maladies of the body and the soul were prospering as was the bubonic plague.

While the doctor/ priest role was prominent in Europe, in China, Confucius was outlining principles of good medicine, similar to Hippocrates of Greece, but with fewer specific value assumptions. Confucius was clear that the medical practitioner was primarily a man of virtue. The Confucian doctor did not need look to a fellowship to decipher an ethical dilemma. The Chinese doctor looked to his conscience and wisdom. Confucius was clear that a good doctor first had to be a man of the highest quality.

Secularization in medicine began to return around the 17th century. The essential Greek component of friendship, an appreciation of the patient's non-material self, carried through as did the notion of professional virtue. However, as the advances in the 19th and 20th century science began to propel the doctor to a more rarefied intellectual status, this friendship component, which for so many years, and through so many cultures had been deemed essential to the doctor patient relationship, began to wither.

A distancing of the learned medical practitioner and the patient settled in. Medical schools became dazzled by their science. A sense of loftiness crept into the profession and new doctors began to be taught a more detached material-only approach to medicine. Advances in medical sciences through this period were phenomenal and physicians built fiefdoms around which dark forests of ignorance became the patients' habitat. For a while the patient was designated to a place among the mushrooms, where intellectual light was banished. However, as we've come into the 21st century, medical knowledge is now available to patients. As a result, there has never been more dissatisfaction with the drawbridge up healthcare model.

Patients know more and want more. They see a deficit. The essential elements of the profession as described by the Greeks: friendship in its fullest definition, seems to be missing. The Confucian confidence in the doctor, as he of the highest morality, is gone. Trust and respect have been busted by knowledgeable patients discovering error and ignorance in their barber surgeons. The Ancient Indian notion of the doctor as virtuous and lofty has disappeared. The academies of medicine have been slow to adapt to a democratic model of healthcare.

What has made this void so clear to today's patients? They are more educated. They have the latest advances regarding their malady and many are visiting doctors with a collaborative imperative. They expect to engage in a conversation. Some are receiving the latest papers on their illness, with it popping up in real time as they sit in their doctors' waiting rooms. The doctor does not have the results of the study, but the patient does. The patients of this medical age are not waiting. They are not patient and a new name for those in compromised wellness will no doubt evolve.

Flux has brought the doctor patient relationship to its new capacity. There must be something informative in the metrics of that flux or in the variables attached to the vector. There is. It is education and today it is the immediacy of information through social media. The possibility of real-time biomedical connections to our doctors, information, information values, along with disease explosion in both chronic and acute types has brought an urgency to patients' behavior and doctors must adjust to these developments.

The practice of medicine is changing and this is essential and true to its nature. Sounds a bit like friendship, alive and moving, creating itself in flux and building from there. There is also a new consciousness that goes way beyond self and flows into the collective.

There is a new collective and a new notion of friendship and professionalism. Ideas about expertise and education have changed as has a tolerance for the dominant and subordinate social dynamic. There could be wellness in that and we are about to find out.

Appreciating Our Essential Professionals

We've all had teachers. We have opinions about teachers. We've had teachers who've changed our lives in all sorts of ways. We've had teachers for many years. Some of us have children who have teachers. Some of us are teachers.

We've all had doctors. Some of us have had many doctors. We have opinions about doctors. We've had good doctors and bad doctors we think. We've had doctors who've helped us with all sorts of things and we've had doctors who didn't help. Some of us have children who have doctors. Some of us are doctors.

Do teachers feel valued? Do doctors feel valued? In the ancient world both the teacher and the doctor were esteemed members of the community. Sometimes they were the same person. Aristotle was the esteemed tutor of Alexander the Great. Hippocrates was a doctor and a teacher. Leonardo da Vinci was a teacher of doctors through his anatomical studies and he was said to have played doctor.

In the early days of Canada and the United States the teacher might be found living in a teensy room in an isolated schoolhouse, dependent on the benevolence of a nearby farmer to throw some wood his way. He or she was often seen slightly in the social misfit category. Teaching was not a role for a respectable married man or woman. A doctor might live in town and have a horse and cart. He would definitely have an esteemed role in the community. He might get paid with a pail of milk or maybe not at all, but he was usually revered.

Teachers often don't feel valued by society as a whole. What causes these feelings of disaffection? Let's look at the earthly trappings and today's metrics of success. It is quite usual for a teacher to have no personal space at their work. Most professionals have an office, cubicle or at least a desk to call their own. Teachers usually do not have an office.

They may have an office which they share with colleagues but it is no place where they can call their doctor's office to privately receive medical results or to have a discussion with their spouse about the fundamentals of marriage. There isn't even a cubicle in my memory bank of teacher work spaces. An office worker may have a cubicle that serves to cut out the white noise of their day. It's a little safe cave, popularly ridiculed, but often a solace to an individual.

Does a teacher have a desk? Well yes, most teachers have a desk, but it is often in a place where others drop things. It is in a place where people often hover. Students lean on it and inadvertently leave bits of flotsam. A parent, who ventures into the realm, looks down over the surface of the desk. She scans for evidence of her child like a starving eagle looking for a vole across a desert expanse. Even the most revered teacher's desk is often as exposed as the scraped earth itself. The teacher's salary is modest. The teacher has few company provided gizmos to call her own.

The successful executive of the corporate world is treated to top-of-the line laptops and handheld devices. Sure these devices make them more effective, and in many ways more servile, but let's face it, we all love our company-provided devices and communications plans. Teachers usually do not have these toys. The executive's salary is substantial and maybe incentive based. The clothing of the trade for the executive involves sharp suits and stylish shoes. The teacher seeks a level of personal style, comfort and affordability, ie. wash and wear.

Doctors and teachers are in a curious relationship to each other. They both perform foundational services to our communities. We cannot prosper without them. We need such a great number of teachers that the very importance of their service has diminished the quality of their work lives. We ask more and more of them. They feel less and less valued as the schools in which they work become shabbier and the supplies are challenged by budget cuts. Sometimes the more they do, the less they feel valued. Some get cranky and some get resentful.

Have doctors too become victims of their own importance? We certainly need doctors. Historically, medical training was designed to keep us patients at bay. A certain mystique was encouraged. The doctor was trained to maintain a position of loftiness. The problem now is that patients have more information. Just like the teacher's desk we are hovering over their diagnosis and treatments with the scope of search engines. We now scan our doctors like the eagle for the vole. We see mousey twitches about the nose and recognize they are people, who sometimes don't know.

How are doctors feeling? It was once thought that a medical life provided all sorts of material trappings. In those metrics of today do doctors feel like success stories? Do they feel valued? I've heard they feel under siege. We are all so critical. They are just practicing the medicine that they learned. Do we know how expensive it is to run a doctor's office? They have hard costs of equipment, and space. They must deal with staff and accounting. They have insurance. They don't have just any insurance, they have malpractice insurance. They are buried in paperwork.

The other thing that doctors now have that teachers have been putting up with, since the proverbial kid in grade four shot the ink pellet off the sling shot and hit every Miss Purdy on her paddy, is scorn. Just like teachers, doctors are now confronted with all of us passing judgment on their work. We think we know something. I suppose we do and we're not use to knowing this much about our health, and we're not using that knowledge gracefully sometimes. Sometimes, we're not using that knowledge wisely, and sometimes we forget the limits of our own Internet medical training. Maybe, when everybody adopts some humility it will be easy to look the other in the eye and respond, "Now that sounds worth considering. Where did you read it?"

It won't matter who delivered this question. Each will understand the availability of the question as a reflection of the information burst of our times. They'll direct each other to the source. They'll be curious. Then looking each other in the eye, they'll carve an action plan and a way to work together that satisfies the partnership needs on both sides of the stethoscope. The patient will recognize the doctor is more equipped to evaluate the information. The doctor will recognize the patient is bringing something that might be useful to the equation.

We all need to understand that there are essential roles in any community and we need to support the people who've assumed them, developed an expertise, and who maybe even felt a vocation to do so.

So let's take an apple or something for the teacher and when you go to your doctor recognize, even though she didn't see that relevant article that burst on the web overnight, it doesn't mean your confidence in her should be shaken. Discuss the findings. Make an assessment of your professional relationship and if it's a good one, build from there. If it's not a good one fix it if you can, and if you can't, keep looking for the right fit. But now that we're sort of grown up, let's not fire any more ink balls at our Grade Three teacher, Miss Worthy, and let's be, neither timid nor hostile, but truthful and engaged in the office of Dr. Wonder. Members of both professions will benefit as will the public they serve.

Share the Infamy

Because it's the common burden of a new thinker I offer the following rich association.

"He was despised. Despised and rejected. A man of sorrow and acquainted with grief. Acquainted with grief." — Isaiah 1iii,3,6

This morning a scientist was denied funding for his research in a particular specialty. It was not explained to him why he was denied. His grant applications were crudely rebuffed. He was not disheartened. He will press on.

The 19th century's Dr. Ignatius Semmelweis insisted that his medical students wash their hands after working with cadavers and before assisting in the delivery of babies. At his hospital one in six women were dying from complications after childbirth. He understood the likely connection of infection. Alas, Dr. Semmelweis' wisdom was not appreciated. Hand washing was considered much too silly and simplistic. The Dr. was so ridiculed by his peers that his mental state unhinged and he spent the final years of his life in an insane asylum.

Charles Darwin was caricatured in *Punch* and *London Illustrated News*. His theories were considered fantastical and far-fetched if not blasphemous. They met popular culture and they were disassembled with a certain enthusiasm and mockery. The press worked it. His personal features were caricatured including his hirsuteness and high brow. Naturally, he was selected in these cartoons as ape.

He took it with a smile telling his friends that he saved each and every one of those drawings. He knew his findings were good.

"He gave his back to the smiters
And his cheeks to them
that plucked off the hair
He hid not his face
from shame and spitting."

"This is junk," responded an anonymous gatekeeper of a purse to the application of Dr. XY. However, like his predecessors and many who came after him, Dr. XY persisted.

"(1)He hid not his face(2) from shame (3,4,1). (2and)from shame (a)and Spitting (2,3,4).

Handel's version

Now, XY is recipient of many awards and holds the Head post at a pre-eminent university. The Board for the funding body which had originally rejected his work eventually understood the research as innovative, and yes, risky but with immense potential. They decided the possible rewards were too great to deny. In their decision making they discussed the level of risk and the potential for return. Possibility won, and the funding was granted.

Dr. XY's stature went full circle. First he was ridiculed, then he was exalted, now he is facing scorn again. For a while he was recognized as one of the foremost geneticists and ground-breaking researchers in the world. His work helped scientists gather a full picture of diseases and this facilitated improved diagnostic and therapeutic approaches. Now these findings are being questioned.

Often, these things often don't have gentle endings. Misery can be the reward for someone who steps away from the norm.

"He was cut off out of the land of the living
 for the transgression of thy people
was he stricken."
Isaiah 1iii,8

Semmelweis just wanted people to wash their hands before treating patients, and he was ridiculed with the final insult in his own poor medical treatment. He became infected after receiving treatment for an injury. Semmelweis died of septicaemia after being locked in a mental asylum. Alas, hand washing was just not dignified enough for endorsement by the medical societies and he was fully ridiculed. Besides a fellow named Hippocrates had already explained infection as an imbalance of the Humours.

His story and this image is perhaps a good argument for maintaining a sense humour. Admittedly, there aren't many chuckles in Handel's *Messiah* libretto either. Seems Darwin was right about a lot of things. One thing is clear, a tolerance for infamy seems to be a useful character trait for an innovator.

What is a Barber Shop?

In the 80's there was a place on Parliament Street in Toronto. It was everything that innovative seemed not. It was dusty. It was staid. The dial on the radio station hadn't been touched in, maybe, decades. Sam ran the joint.

I was a kid writing one-act plays and I'd hit on Sam's as the place where something amazing was happening. What that something was, was nothing. I loved it. I'd walk by late at night and look through the painted lettered window that read Sam's Hairstyling. The sign on the door still read OPEN and it seemed if I tried the door, I'd be able to let myself in and climb up onto one of the black vinyl chairs.

OPEN

My apartment up the street was filled with cockroaches and the sounds of arguing neighbours. I'd moved in with the hope of expanding my sensibilities. The halls were yellow with nicotine and around the doors loitered prowling men with wagging tongues. I'd leave with my notebook and pen and stay away for hours on end. I spied on Sam.

Every morning Sam arrived with three tabloid newspapers under his arm. He'd flick on the lights of his shop and in a fluid motion turn the sign from OPEN to CLOSED. He always had a coffee in a styrofoam cup and he'd place it on the counter that ran in front of the mirror of his four cutting chairs.

Then he'd place down the tabloids for the use of clients who he knew would come and wait. He tossed the previous day's tabloids in the garbage bin which was next to the big black pay phone. There was no recycling then.

Sam would then climb up onto one of his swiveling black barber chairs, pick up his coffee and swing the chair to face the door. He'd sit there. He'd sip his coffee. He'd look out. He'd drink some more. He'd stare. Then he'd spot someone on the street. He'd lean forward to see as much as possible without getting out of the chair. They'd pass. The excitement was over. He'd relax. He'd sit back. He'd sip his coffee. He'd drink. He'd stare.

Then a great commotion of activity would fall upon Sam's Hairstyling. A guy would walk up to the joint carrying a bundle of linen and a clipboard. He'd walk into Sam's. He'd toss the linen on the chair next to Sam.

"Morning, Harry."

"Morning, Sam"

"Thanks, Harry."

"You're welcome, Sam."

Sam would nod. Harry would nod. Harry would leave. Sam would resume his pose.

This is fantastic, I thought. I watched from my seat on the curb on the other side of the street and I made notes. I'd become quite overt and Sam had stopped even noticing me sitting there. I'd become a part of the scenery. So the day I walked in and asked if I could visit. Sam just shrugged and said, "OK."

After the linen delivery Gordy the Parking Metreman would arrive. He'd always act like he was going to walk past. He would walk just past the door then he'd dip back, as if in after-thought. He'd look both ways, flip his ticket pad closed, look up and down the street again, and then he'd enter.

"Hi Gordy."

"Hi Sam. Can I get ya a coffee?"

Sam would hold up his cup to show Gordy that he was in possession. Gordy always offered Sam a coffee, and always knew that Sam already had a coffee. I wondered what would happen if Sam didn't have a coffee one day. I think Gordy would have become quite discombobulated. He'd probably leave and never come back. That didn't happen though, and life in Sam's Hairstyling unfolded.

"I've got one. Thanks."

Gord nods. Sam nods. Gord leaves.

Sam stands. He goes and turns on the green plastic radio. He reaches to adjust the dial, but thinks better of it. While his back is turned a customer walks in. Sam turns. He sees the guy. He walks over to his kit and pulls out a vinyl barber apron and drapes it over the customer. He announces, "Mr James O'Dowd."

James O'Dowd sits in the chair as if he's sat in it a thousand times. Mr. O'Dowd is silent. He looks into the mirror. Sam starts the snip, snip, snipping. No questions are needed, but I get the sense Sam is performing for me, because I've told him I'm writing a play.

Sam: "How long have you lived around here Jimmy?"

O'D:"Oh jeez, Sam! I grew up here. I've always been here.

Sam: "That right?"

Sam's not really asking a question. He's more acknowledging O'Dowd's reply.

Sam: "Read today's paper?"

O'D: "Nope, not yet."

Sam: "Well, look at here."

Sam grabs the tabloid and puts it on the table in front of the mirror. He stabs at it with his scissors and slides it over so O'Dowd can see.

Sam: "A body found in the brick works this morning. A young guy."

O'D: "Jeez. Ya. Look at that. When I was a kid I used to go down there and watch the prisoners. ...during the war, I mean. They used to live in quanset huts down there.

Sam: Ya...in the winter. Jeez it would have been cold!"

(snip...snip....sn...ip)

Sam: "What kind of huts?"

O'D: "Quanset huts. They, the prisoners, used to make things. You know? Craft-type things."

Sam: "Like what?"

(snip...comb..comb...snip)

O'D: "Like rings made out of toothbrushes and paste of chewed up paper. People used to buy them from them or trade them for cigarettes or something.

Sam: "My friend's father was imprisoned there because he was a member....

A young man with longish hair comes in. He sits down. Sam and O'Dowd turn to look at him. Jimmy O'Dowd doesn't stop talking.

...of the socialist party."

Sam pauses. Drops his scissors to his side and turns to the new customer.

"Hi, Young Fellow."

O'D: "It was Bill's dad."

Sam: "Oh ya? His son comes in here. Bill's son. I cut his hair."

O'D : "Ya? Well, my friend Tom was the oldest boy and they arrested him too. The kid and the father...all because the father was a card carrying member of the socialist party. It was Bill's Dad."

snip . snip . snip...

I sat there listening to all this and saw that outside the store there was a certain 80's style to things but inside, time was all confused. It was just post-war. That's all a person could say...sometime, post-war.

O"D: "The kid said, ' Let me out and I'll join the army.' So they did. The father, though. He was in from '42. Oh, I just don't know. I just don't know. It was hard on the kids."

Sam: "What happened in the end, James..to all the prisoners?"

Sam finishes and gets his big brush and swings it all over James O'Dowd's shoulders.

O'D: "Oh, I imagine they shipped a lot of them back..especially the ones to Germany but some of them stayed."

He stands as he says this. He adjusts his pants. He pulls them up a long journey above his waist. The change rattles. He pays Sam.It's seven dollars a cut.

"Ok."

The men nod in mutual satisfaction about the transaction.

"Bye, Sam."

"Bye, James O'Dowd."

The day goes on and these sorts of conversations play out. I write it all down. I wander by the shop in the middle of the night and see the sign reading OPEN. I wonder. I know Sam's not illiterate because he read about the body in the brickworks. I think that, perhaps, he's a pattern follower.

Perhaps one day the sign got forgotten. Maybe Sam was sick or there had been an emergency. One day Sam must have missed flipping the sign and then from then on, when he was back to his routine he just went back to the usual flipping pattern. Only then the sign was reversed.

I always wondered whether Sam was just incapable of breaking his routine. Would it have been upsetting to him to not flip the lights and then the sign on one day? Maybe Sam was just playing a little joke on the world. There might have been something clever about Sam. His business hadn't changed for years and years and it was a booming enterprise. The one chair was never empty, except in the nights when my nose was pressed to the glass. There was always a customer or two waiting. The conversation always seemed slow and interesting. There was nothing innovative about this place. All around new stores popped up and stylists and cafes boasted a hipsterville but with money attitude. Not so, Sam's Hairstyling. He was constant. There was nothing disruptive. It was the very stuff of an institution. It was a $7 haircut.

I continued to live in the neighbourhood for a bit and then moved a long way away for a number of years. Every now and then I'd pass through and I'd see Sam's surrounded by unrecognizable boutiques, new buildings and well-dressed thirty year olds. Then a long time later I took a nostalgic drive past and Sam's was gone.

Was Sam's cleverness, his innovative genius, constancy? When all was changing and denying the value of what is a barber shop, was Sam's the only institute recognizing its place and value? How did Sam, if he did, understand so well the particular essence his establishment contributed to the neighbourhood? I think Sam was equal parts humility and pride and a balance of these features created bedrock. Maybe it was simple and honest. Sam put on no pretense. He was what he was. He offered it without affectation. He enjoyed what he did and he, maybe, understood it with a little touch of humour.

He marked his store closed when it was open and open when it was closed. He always had his coffee and he let everyone else find their way in and out of his realm, even the metre man Gordy who's joy in life was snagging the cars.

After the early morning coffee salutation Gordy would reappear intermittently throughout the day. For a period he would lurk in Sam's doorway with his ticket pad. He'd stand there staring at half charged parking metres. He'd stare and stare. Every now and then he'd spring spider-like out of the corner of his web, Sam's front door, and plant a fat ticket on a vulnerable car.

(snip. ..snip...snip...)

Sam wouldn't say a thing but maybe chuckle just a bit.

So, when is constancy innovative? Is it when humility and pride balance? Is this where honesty is found?

POLITICAL

Great Limits Great Power

Great Limits Come With Great Power, Ex-Candidate Finds. How to fill a phrase with meaning? The lesson was offered in the *Sunday New York Times* page 22 dated January 24th, 2009 with this headline juxtaposed against a panel of photographs: Obama surrounded by the press, and beneath that, Obama signing executive orders regarding the closing of Guantanamo, but here's the real kicker, the bottom of the panel, Obama returning to the office after visiting the State Department.

There is the new President of the United States, a sophisticated man, an educated man, a charismatic man, a man holding unprecedented stature for a huge percentage of the US population as a virtual American messiah. Now look at the photograph. For those familiar with the world of the southern United States, its artists and culture, it may have caused a spilling of the morning coffee and a quick adjustment of the reading specs.

Attending a South Carolina auction house of fine art and treasures, for me, was a bi-monthly lesson in Americana. What was clear to a foreigner in the South is that the times of slavery and the civil war are very much alive in memory and in the emotional timbre of the population. Artifacts and artwork of the slavery period were commonly on the block.

Artists Alfred Hutty and Carew Rice depicted the African American. Hutty became known for etchings produced in Charleston. Rice took up a Victorian technique and created two-dimensional silhouettes in black and white. In both styles, the renderings sometimes exaggerated physical traits and the subjects were placed in stereotypical roles. These works led to a world of PhD theses on the topic of slavery, art, and the American experience. There were almost always knarly overhanging trees in the images. In the more current works of Kara Walker the figure is hanging from the tree.

Look at this photograph of Barack Obama which appeared in the *New York Times* on January 24th, 2009 by Charles Dharapak courtesy of the *Associated Press*.

There he is under the gnarly tree that, in shape, could be any of the many that line the marsh land on the inland waterways that fed the South Carolina plantations and under which the slave cabins were often situated. There he is in silhouette in a posture like that of the caricature in a Hutty depiction. Hutty's character walked in rags, and here Obama's suit, the suit of the US Commander-in-Chief, flows in no less communion with his backdrop, The White House, than the Hutty clothing does with the back drop of the marsh. There is a leaning in the gait of the Hutty character that is remarkably similar to that of Obama's. The lean is one of motion and perhaps, burden.

What does this say to us? This reader when first seeing these Hutty, Rice depictions in that South Carolina auction house, as a white woman, felt strangely complicit in the objectification and strangely humiliated by the compositions. This photograph of Barack Obama, so clearly comparable to the silhouette or etching style is a brilliant reminder of the pathos of the journey for all Americans in the African American experience.

If an accident of similarity by the photographer or the *Times* editors, it is an accident of brilliance like many accidents that advance us in the world of thinking. If it was a deliberate tactic designed to tweak our consciousness it is a clever use of the medium of print journalism, if a touch metaphoric for the trade. Either way it is a happening that ought to be embraced as it advances the culture out of the embarrassing past and into the promising future.

Deep South, 1932 by Alfred Hutty/(American, 1877-1954) Drypoint on Paper/©Image Courtesy of the Gibbes Museum of Art/Carolina Art Assoication, 1955.05.0010

Now I want a Hutty or Rice to hang on my wall. A version of the Hutty image was on sale in South Carolina, at Charlton Hall Auctions in February 2007 with a house pre-estimate of $2 -$3,000. I don't know where the gavel fell. Damnation! What a celebration! I wish I bought it.

Fooling the Electorate

It happens. Someone who campaigns for change is often, at first, well-received. Sometimes they're even celebrated. Lately there is a lot of talk about advancing systems and social structures, a new healthcare model and a new information architecture. Leaders who try to follow through with The New usually face resistance. In some cases, change occurs simply because the status quo will not hold. In some cases the forward thinking Leader is vilified or turfed out.

Is courage required on the part of any leader? Where do designations of bravery fit into the political world? People often attack the policy and personal life of the visionary who tries to bring change. How much bravery is required to advance new ways? Are bravery and innovation linked?

It seems bravery and change come together when an idea is ahead of its time. Maybe bravery is a component of innovation. As time passes, and if an idea is a solid one, societal momentum moves toward the new way naturally, and then what was once innovative is now just a function of momentum. Bravery separates out from the idea. So as the x axis is time and the y axis is bravery, the line descends.

So maybe the brave leader, with innovation as a goal, needs to be clever, rather than brave. The leader needs to fool the electorate that what is being suggested is at worst at little nudge, but really, the good ole way of doing things. Does every elected innovator have to fool a constituency in order to get past one of the more stifling aspects human nature; fear of change?

We can complain about the song and dance that we see our elected officials performing, but maybe we're just collectively adolescent enough that nothing can happen without the circus act.

Mistakes and The Castrati at the Hockey Game

It was Saturday morning in the rink. I stood up on the bench between two team Dads. We all had guys on the ice and were each engaged in the particular rapture that parents know. It's about our children's pleasures and it comes with the ecstatic thrill of their successes and the engulfing chill of their difficulties. We parents remember the sensual acuity of childhood. That childhood alertness is described by Wordsworth in *Ode: Intimations of Immortality*.

There was a time when meadow, grove, and stream,
The earth, and every common sight,
To me did seem
Apparelled in celestial light,
The glory and the freshness of a dream
It is not now as it hath been of yore; –
Turn wheresoe'er I may,
By night of day,
The things which I have seen I now can see no more.

The parent enjoys a reminder of the naïve experience of which the poet describes. It is different from a more experiential clarity that comes through art or romantic love or maybe an earthly achievement in any iconic game.

Wordsworth's poem carries a heavy melancholia over the loss of it that comes with adulthood. Did Wordsworth have kids? Yes, he had six. Maybe that's how he could see the loss so clearly, and maybe that's how he was able to describe the early dream so well.

There we parents stood on the benches, the ice bright and white and ribboned with blue and red. Sure it was probably brighter and whiter and more ribbony for the boys. Certain smells were maybe more distinct, and the sounds more crisp for them. Senses do fade with age. Standing up high on the benches made us parents more vibrantly in tune with the game, and it also brought us a few feet closer to the mean small heaters in the concrete arena.

The ice was fast and the opponents were all over our team. We held our own, though, and cheered as our boys passed and took shots on net. They dodged and deeked out their opponents, and they busted out at full speed with clear ice in front of them. The parents shouted and hollered. The Dad's voices were huge and poured out of them, filling the rink. Standing there between two Dads, I thought, "Holy volume"! These were two Dads of no vocal training and their voices amazed me.

"Go!"

Pass it! Pass it!

"Ya! "

It turned my mind to the Castrati of the Bel Canto period of voice. No wonder, in the quest for the greatest voice, the voice that would fill the halls with size and sweetness, the impresarios did not look to develop the girls. They looked to the boys. Chop. Chop. Yes. The boys were relieved of their paraphernalia. This meant that as they grew they still had the physical size of chest, lungs, sinuses, palate, thighs and all the components of the body that make up the instrument like the case and board of the piano. They did not have the involvement of hormones that caused the thickening of the vocal chords nor the disruption of pliability, nor the rasping and deepening of the tone.

So there I was standing in the rink thinking how these two Dads would have been fabulous castrati had they been subjected to the innovators of the 18th century and supposing they'd been singled out in the choir. Instead the Dads stood in the rink cheering for their progeny. I watched the game and even though my mind wandered a bit, I saw every save.

"What a stop!"

"Right off the blocker!"

The other thing about this pair that was interesting is that they are both innovators in their field.

"Nice pass!"

"Did you see that?"

One guy travels internationally leading carbon discussion and is building an expertise and political suasion on the subject. The other holds an elected office. He has attempted to move an entire electorate in a new direction. He has operated an environmental mandate from increasingly influential political posts. He's taken profound steps, nurtured technology and seen it through to implementation. His political efforts go years deep and I expect will continue for years to come. They both have innovation on their minds as a matter of urgency.

Operatic innovation of the 18th century involved the chopping of the testicoli . That method of extending the boy soprano's career was very successful. It was justified in biology and promoted in greed. It was cold-hearted and often done for the glory of the family or the church. It was not done for the poor boys. Of course, the big stars probably had good lives. The boys whose voices did not raise them to stardom must have suffered long past the slice.

Looking back on today, especially on our missteps, we should be able to see there was a reason to forge ahead on any chosen path. It would be good to think a compass of decency will prevent cruelty to humans, animals and earth. Hopefully, today's political decisions and innovations won't have required anyone giving up their orbs. In fact, as we all know, it is more likely that said planets will be a sizeable requirement to achieving next steps, and not excluding the cosmic power that is inseparable from the ovary.

Our boys have a game tonight. It'll be cold in the rink so I better wear my big coat. The voices will fill the arena. I'll go and hold a cup of tea for warmth and watch my child. All of us parents attending will feel the spirit of the game with just a hint, or not, of Wordsworth's " glory and freshness of the dream".

The parents, the two aforementioned Dads will cheer and holler encouragement. I'll listen. It must have been incredibly strange to hear those fabricated and original bel canto sopranos. There must have been an eeriness to the sound that told the audience that this, as innovation, was wrong. The contortion probably jarred the senses even as it thrilled. The Castrato was not natural and probably disturbing to human instinct. I hope future innovation that rubs against the natural world will be obvious to us, and disappear as oddities of a brief age like genetically modified flax.

In the meantime intact Dads watch hockey. The Mums and Dads feel the spirit of their children, and occasionally glance at the incoming messages on the handhelds that feed back to them a calibration of their tests in the world.

The dreamy exaltation of youth, the awareness of adulthood, some smarts and a barometer of decency seem essential for true innovation. We won't recognize all of our mistakes but hopefully we will catch some.

The game is over. Just in time for me, as my toes were starting to freeze and everybody's inboxes, wikis, blogs, social media postings are primed or jammed and probably not fully accessible inside the cement block arena.

Groupthink

Biting the hand that feeds you is considered an unwise act, unless you work with the Health Strategy Innovation Cell. I think us Cellies like it, at least we like a little nibbling, and so I want to roll over a few thoughts on the topic of Healthcamp Toronto. If I disappear like Deng Xiaoping you'll know why.

I'm thinking about China. Actually what brings me to thoughts of China is the phenomenon of groupthink. I've been trying to form an opinion about groupthink. It's referenced everywhere these days in social media and trending. I've been trying to come to a dramatic example of groupthink in action.

The Proletarian Cultural Revolution comes to mind as described in Nien Cheng's, *Life and Death in Shanghai*. The author describes organized groups of young people, The Red Guard, tearing through the city burning books, smashing ancient porcelain treasures and even more ancient musical instruments, urinating on early dynasty furniture and walloping intellectuals about the ears.

"As they crowded into the hall, one of them knocked over a pot of jasmine on a Fen T'sai porcelain stool. The tiny white blooms scattered on the floor were trampled by their impatient feet...

'We are the Red Guards. We have come to take revolutionary action against you.'"

Was this an example of groupthink? Well, it was certainly group behaviour, but the extent to which it can be called groupthink is unclear. Healthcamp Toronto galvanized by my Cell colleagues attracted a committed group of participants. All were invited to offer opinion and share concerns on patient-focused healthcare issues.

The goal of any Healthcamp is to provide a live and cyber gathering place for healthcare discussion to launch ideas into action -- in an organic, unstructured way. There are a lot of people who have dedicated much thinking to patient-led change, and it seems that it can only be fruitful to bring them together.

Is there trouble with this? No. This only becomes troubling if the tone of the conversation becomes hyperbolic. It is only a concern if everyone agrees and no one listens. It is a concern if a vocal few move a majority of the participants in a way that is only emotional and unflavoured with intellectual temperance.

There are measurable changes in the world of medicine, and there is a growing culture of collaboration among professionals. With the social media available to us today, it seems not only promisingly effective for us to communicate with each other, but it also seems so easy it's immoral not to do so. Here's why: each of us owns a body and a certain expertise. There is not a layperson among us on this matter. So, in a forum like this we may have a number of experts expressing highly informed and experientially biased points of view.

I think any moderator of a successful Healthcamp will need a strategy for spotting an insidious drift as well as a positive wave, and a moderator may need to bring in structure (within an "unstructured" context) to challenge the flow. It's not that a consensus is always wrong; it's just that consensus is usually not revelatory and sometimes it's downright nutty. I think there should be aspirations for dissent, debate, and thought building, but no conclusions, please.

In his book *The Chinese*, author John Fraser notes that Mao's state publishing house always presented his commentary in bold letters. Mr. Fraser also writes that in some editions of the Bible the words of Christ were printed in red. This was to exalt the speakers. Well, the moderator of Healthcamp does not need to be exalted, but I think a moderator might want to have some sort of distinguishing "otherness" in order to draw attention to worrisome signs of agreement that grow out of nothing other than the charisma of the crowd. Is there to be a moderator at all? Can a crowd ever moderate itself? Is there such a thing as too much egalitarianism? Proponents of Wikipedia™ probably would deny such a notion, but I wonder. Untempered crowds sure spook me.

Healthcamp is based on an idea that getting people together to talk is a lively, dynamic way to expand ideas and a wise and informed way to nurture policy. The ideal at the foundation of this is probably a belief in the value of the opinions of others. Mao didn't want to hear the ideas of others, he just wanted them to indulge his own thoughts. The Proletarian Cultural Revolution could be said then to be a time of 'groupthunk' where ideas were stuck. Still, stale, stunk, or, as Mao was quoted, on the matter of The Gang of Four, "Sh*t. Wide of the mark."

Healthcamp Toronto was part of a bottom up Reformation, not a top-down revolution.

Iran, Innovation, Mistakes, Fundamentals – an archaeological consideration

Summer, 2009…Iran. The streets are filled with people wanting change. How can westerners understand what they want? We look at them and wonder how they can be so brave. We think the jails are filled with good people. Are they? We think the government will open fire any time? We'll see. We graft western ideals onto a culture we don't understand? It is now being said the movement is largely a women's movement. What does this mean? Common thinking would have us believe that each of the women we see on the news is at risk of being beaten by their fathers, husbands, brothers or neighbours. What do we know? The protests continue. Are the women in terrible peril? In our ignorance we combine the cultures of all of the countries of the Middle East. Saudia Arabia becomes Iraq becomes Syria becomes Iran etc.

It has been written that the many invaders of Persia became Persian in spirit. Persia was once vast and far-reaching. Now, some use the name to speak of Iran. Many of the invaders of Persia attempted to impose their culture on the land and instead they became absorbed and transformed by it. Alexander the Great married Roxana in what was said to be both a political and a love match. He also organized a mass marriage for his army and out of these conquerors came many new devoted Persians. Sure, you have to wonder what the women thought of those unions.

The latest influx of people into Iran, about 300 years ago were Arabs. Perhaps this latest insurrection is the final prodding of these cultural occupiers toward the classical Persian ways.

Persian culture even predated the nearby Mesopotamia and what is cited as the first literate culture of peoples. If all cultures that have come into the new Persia are melding toward the original culture of the place, is this illustrated by an ongoing shift toward underpinnings? Is this one reason for the ongoing tumult? Will the creation of a new Iran, an innovative Iran, come from recognition and embracing of underpinnings? Are the people of Iran being pulled as if by a natural force toward their fundamental identity, in fact all of our fundamental identities in the establishment of original

101

human society? Does this demand a shedding of what is not true, but has been applied to the country's daily life? Do they see these applications weighing on their culture rather than feeding it? A whale encrusted with barnacles loses its luster. Persian poetry ever florid suggests that Persian identity is found in an on going attempt to return to an original beauty.

The collective West needs to understand, that it is not western ways that will flower in Iran. Strife may be the natural condition of Iran as the society ever attempts to move toward an ideal. Maybe the better of the original Persian values will one day be recovered and validated. It is more likely that even these values are as moveable as the individuals who seek them.

Could examining how the present has strayed from foundations inform innovation? As is necessarily human, do we make mistakes and grow in directions that are not sustaining of our values, only to discover a need to backtrack and rebuild based on a more refined understanding of what is foundational. Is back tracking always difficult and sometimes violent? Is this from where innovation comes? Can we refit our foundations? Is innovation to be excavated out of the mistakes that we graft onto ourselves, and does progress come after the exfoliation? Do unrest, civil strife, violence and subversion become grafted onto our societies when we've made big missteps? It doesn't seem possible that there could be a society founded on an ideal of oppression. People would not have formed into society if it was not happier, more safe and preferable to them. The impetus that formed that society must have come from, some very simple universal themes; basic human need.

My friend is in the hospital. She has almost no nursing care. The helping hand has been given up to the banal tasks of operating a floor and counting materials. The care-giving, the core value of nursing, where she is, has been subsumed.

The starting point of healthcare as a vocation has been to provide comfort, nourishment and healing. How serious is the absence of these fundamentals? Is my friend's experience unique? If not, where has the foundation gone? Are the underpinnings mired over in a crust of busy work?

Perhaps, as in the rich and astonishing Iran, an archaeological initiative is required. Removing the crust that has settled onto healing values and getting to the good true surface of what these values are and making it possible to honour them could awaken a whole new age of compassion.

Apparently, the protestors of Iran did need to fear. Unidentified snipers shot into the crowd. A girl became famous for her death. Secret prisons filled and people disappeared. It seems that the reasons we live in a society are still forgotten by some, in that first of human gathering places near Mesopotamia. The burying of the societal foundation is pushing innovation away.

The War of Northern Aggression

The outburst of South Carolinian Republican Joe Wilson, whom you may remember as the guy who called Obama a liar in the House of Representatives, has led me to pick up the collection of historical essays by the Southern historian C. Vann Woodward, *The Burden of Southern History*.

Another deeply embedded trait of the Southern [novelist] that has a strong appeal to a historian is their way of treating man not as an individual alone with his conscience or his God...but as an inextricable part of a living history and community, ...

Mr. Woodward might have something to say about the Palmetto State's Congressman as it pertains to his sense of community. Mr. Wilson's method of communication, and more, the response of his constituents, tells us so much about the character of the State and the challenges it faces in order to evolve.

I had the eye-opening pleasure of living in the Midlands of South Carolina for a couple of years. It is a curious place in that its most influential citizens seem to be stuck in another time and place. This makes it an informative backdrop to the topic of innovation. My first visit there was in November when my husband and I were considering the move. After a lovely dinner party we stepped outside into warm air of a quality I hadn't before experienced. I could not distinguish what made it unique. It was somehow in the slight warm breeze but that wasn't the all of it. It wasn't the wine at dinner of which there was only a tempered amount. Perhaps it had something to do with the curious organic essence of the swamp suspended in the atmosphere. I could feel something sumptuous on my skin. I breathed. I wondered what it would be like to live in this air. I would find out.

The Southerners collective sense of self seems to be highly conflicted. I noticed fairly quickly, and more so as time went by, that there is a curious combination of shame and pride in the South Carolinian. There seemed to be an assumption that people from elsewhere did not respect them. A southern man of some brilliance told me of time spent at a New York law firm. He said something to the effect of,

I could tell they were patronizing me. 'Isn't it cute the way our junior colleague speaks,' he imitated. They thought it enhanced them to have a Southerner, but I could tell they didn't respect me or where I was from. I decided to come home to my family, and be with my aging parents. I wanted to live with my own people.

I was really quite shocked to hear this man underestimate his place at the firm. It seemed inconceivable to me that he wouldn't have been valued for his legal skill because his mind was acute. I saw this attitude play out again and again with both the capable people and the simply entitled.

They think we are just a bunch of dumb-ass southerners.

I'd really never heard this sort of thing before, and I had come to the State with no knowledge of these sorts of perceptions. Sure I knew of the history, but I had not the slightest awareness of how alive and visceral were the feelings of oppression among the affluent whites.

They came here and they burnt our houses, said the stung fifty-five year old child of cotton, his eyes flashing and searching to see if I understood.

Woodward references Herbert Marshall McLuhan on the topic of Southern character and southern literature who cites, T.S. Stribling writing of,

...the chain of wrongs and violences out of which life has been molded.

The Southerners prided themselves on a heightened sense of gentility. *Yes Ma'am*, poured from all and sundry. At first I thought this was charming. Later I discovered that it was a reflex that came to signify a collective sense of societal betterness. It also became an excuse for certain unbecoming behaviours. It was as though, with the institutions of Ma'am and Church all things were excusable.

If a person disagreed on a matter trite or profound, a Southerner of a certain caste would nod and listen. He did not offer a suggestion or different point of view. That would have been considered impolite, especially with a foreigner. To engage in collaborative thinking with someone is to bring them into your world. This Southerner protects his world.

There were only three areas of life in which he expressed himself openly: sports, religion and politics. It was there that all the stops and masks of identity fell away. He was hyperbolic in these three areas. Even the most genteel of Southern belles hollered surprisingly t-shirted in team colours and hands-filled with homemade clackers. The preachers on the altar stare down the newcomers to inspect their commitment to the Creed. There is no tolerance for ongoing introspection in these matters. You are for the team or you are not, and you better be for the right team. The banker wants to know if you go to his church. He's not unusual. Everyone wants to know if your religion is their brand. Judaism is sort of tolerated because its roots are deep enough in commerce and industry, because it is so distinctly other and because the history of anti-semitism is so distinctly impolite. Ultimately, though, the Texan stated it thus,

You're either with us, or you're ag'in us.

The Republican in the House shouts out "liar" to the President. At first there were traditional Southerners who thought Mr. Wilson shamed their state in his failure of manners. Soon though, the tide turned. Many of the man's constituents, the members of his team and his church applauded him and offered funds to his and his son's campaigns. He did, after all, stand up to the other, the Northerner. He called him out, and he called Obama before veracity; before God as Mr. Wilson might say. He did not call him out on a matter of ideology, he called the President out on a matter of personal honour . The topic of Mr. Obama's race is no small detail and Jimmy Carter as a Georgian, and a somewhat politically removed one, was free to speak that truth.

The springtime in South Carolina brings a heavenly transition from a grey winter. When the azaleas come out, they cover the state. It's an astonishingly beautiful affair and as they start to fade, the next flowers emerge. Like Joe Wilson's accusation, the orange blossoms and cherry trees, the dogwoods and the lotus flowers burst. In every week of the spring the streets are painted anew. The beauty exhilarates. How is it so that such a tight worldview grows out of this place? When I stepped out my door as the weather warmed and inhaled the beautiful essence of the Jasmine, the *Confederate Jasmine*, as it is known, I could not help but be struck by the sheer troubling magnificence of contradiction.

Does Joe Wilson believe the world can't respect his State because it flies the Confederate flag at the Capital building? Is this why, with fingers pointed and Palmetto cufflinks blaring he looked like Coach Spurrier's most out of place and rabid fan? Perhaps the episode speaks volumes about the Southern tension and the stain of the identity which is the love of the Confederate flag, the implicated Palmetto and the tarnished notion of gentility.

I know Mr. Wilson's Gamecock style caused many reasonable South Carolinians to shake their heads. The man was cartoonish in his manner, and the overt qualities of that genre communicate in a way like no other. There are certainly some locals who agree this has not been a flattering time for South Carolina with a notorious horse-lover and an awol Governor added to the infamy. One thing is clear, as long as the patterns of behavior that the historian Woodward referred to, a sort of protecting one's own, continues, change will not come to the State. As long as any group wears the mantle of oppression as well as an inflated collective sense of self, they will remain inbred, and let's face it, inbreeding of ideas, or not, is famous for creating ugliness.

The world of healthcare can learn from the folly of this inbreeding. Fiefdoms of expertise can be allowed to fall away. Prejudice of practice and process can give over to better ideas even if offered by people outside the traditional areas of medicine.

Note:

The Confederate flag was removed from the top of the South Carolina capital building as recently as July 1, 2000. Many locals had been lobbying for years to have it removed, but any inclined politician knew that doing so would seriously harm prospects for re-election. Finally through lobbying, which in no small way included the influence of the Gamecocks

Football Coach who claimed that it was interfering with recruiting, the flag moved off the building and onto the front lawn; the power of sport, indeed, but only so strong. The flag still flies prominently.

Nelson Mandela Ran Away

"You will marry this girl," said the step-father to the son.
The son owed the man a great deal.
The man was a revered Chief of his tribe

Respected by all
Revered by the community
He'd saved the boy whose father had died
Leaving the mother and child destitute

The woman and child
Were also of the royal line
The Chief saved the boy
from the fall into common life.

In nobility,
he'd provided a home
He sent the boy to school
He loved him as his own

Time passed and the boy grew
Devoted to the chief
The boy excelled in all things
Making the old man proud

The old man could see the boy had greatness
He nurtured him and cultivated his talents
Time passed
The boy was almost a man
The Chief entered into talks
with a neighbouring tribe
The Chiefs agreed
the boy would bond

In a few weeks time
With the other Chief's daughter

The girl was beautiful,
smart and bright
But

The boy did not love her
He was stricken with grief
He suffered a torment as he paced
Thorns from the sand dug in. They stung.

Arrows married with the sand
Pointing creeping many say
Into his feet they filled his veins.
 Moved to his heart and tormented his space.
Thorns

Increasing with the sun each day
Heating sticking a pointy torture
Bloody prickles in his soul
He nursed his inner conflict
The day of the nuptials fast approached
Nearer and nearer did it come
He lay tormented in his bed
He knew it was not to be done

He could not
He must not
He should not marry the girl
He would leave

He arranged for money
He took from his step-father
He fled when the man's back was turned
The boys' sorrow never left him

The old man's pride
Swelled to a fury
He became vindictive

And blocked the railway

So the, boy, he walked
He could not marry the girl

He walked
His feet opened.

Honestly.

Into sores and blisters
He walked
Away
He lost his home. Finally.

He lost
He walked and found
Place
He found himself in Johannesburg
Alone.

He found his way
He was hungry
His clothes were rags
A man gave him a suit of clothes

He wore it every day
After day.
He earned a dollar and bought smoked ham
A strange food he had not seen
What to do with it he wondered.
Cook it please. The butcher smirked?
Embarrassed by his country ways
He opened books

Love found him giddy young delighted
He settled happy in a shack

His palace home
His first requited

He had a child and saw wonder
He put the babe to sleep at night
He studied by precious candlelight
He earned a degree

He met with enlightened people
He practiced law and worked an equal
He didn't marry that daughter of the chief
His step-father remained angry from
Betrayal.
That was done.
He developed his knowledge
He began to understand his country
He argued for the people's rights
He worked
Hard
He loved
Truly

He argued against injustice
He found injustice thrust upon him
He lifted up his people
He inspired

He loved again
Truly done.
He went against his benefactor
In betrayal he had become

He became his own man
He spoke out to his people
He saw the powers of the land
He was imprisoned
He remained true to his ideals

He did not marry that girl
He did not conform out of obligation
Imprisoned

He suffered behind concrete walls
 He walked.
Twenty seven blistered years
He thought.

Had he married the child of the chief
He would have walked free
With many children at his knee
His shade provided. More wives. Broad trees

He would have been revered at home
Happiness and pleasure his village days
Water trickling past him gently, but then,
for certain, turning into acid.

Rain
Betrayal
Obligation
Truth

So he was disobedient. Dry behind stone walls
Defiant. Still.
He lay in chains.
He'd walked away

With bloody feet
He didn't marry that daughter of the chief
He read the books
Of the law

Of the land
And became a man
He was imprisoned

For this crimes
He became iconic
He was freedom
He was honour
He was defiance.

He was released
He changed his country
He had ignored obligation
He would not be coerced
To Action
He changed the world
As a teenager
He defied his parent
As a teenager, he said.
"No"
No, to the ways of old
As a teenager
he became a man
Of his own age.

Innovation from disobedience
A teenage tantrum
authentication
Nelson Mandela ran away.

The Emperor Julian

The Emperor Julian rose to Roman Caesar at Constantinople in 353 AD and later became ruler of all of Rome, until death on the battlefield, in 363 AD.

Called to rule by his murderous cousin Constantius, the very cousin who slaughtered most of his family, he tried to apply the teachings of the philosophers toward the creation of a just society. He moved into Justinian's old digs in Constantinople and immediately attempted to correct the corruption and waste within the government. He attempted to put an end to bribe taking among government officials. He found it distasteful that, for example, a barber to the throne would be granted a large estate, slaves, and many other sundry rewards. He immediately took to dismantling the bloated branches of government toward eliminating wastefulness and gluttony. He strove to set by example and was known in battle to trade the comforts of his position for a footman's bedroll. A surprised foot soldier found himself sleeping in the then Emperor's bed. Julian was in the process of creating a whole new Rome at Constantinople, and after that at Antioch. Ultimately he was hoping to create a Rome of fairness and tolerance.

Julian made the changes quickly. Like any change agent his popularity suffered. He made himself hated by the ruling and middle classes. They saw their perks dwindle away. They saw him as a ruler who was seeking to gain favour with the common people. He stayed in his chambers reading and assessing arguments. He made no efforts toward his ablutions and became unwashed and unshaven in deliberate contrarian asceticism. The people of the court became disgusted by him. He understood this and addressed their repulsion by writing his famous Ode to the Beard Hater. During this time he took up unusual pastimes like writing out the entire Odyssey on the skin of a boa. In all of this, Julian tried to hold himself above the pettiness of gossip and the distemper of interest groups. The more he cordoned himself off with learning, thinking about just government, and personal pursuits, the more the former ruling classes maligned him. The more he studied, and applied theory to his decisions, the more eccentric and unsuited to rule they accused him of being.

He encouraged all critics with tolerance for Christians and Pagans alike. He spoke of acceptance and sought a peaceful society. This level of societal harmony was unheard of under the Christian Emperors that had come before. Pagans had been cruelly treated under those regimes. Julian wanted a different kind of Rome.

This Pagan Emperor, the last of the Pagan Emperors, attempted to rule in fairness and justice. The times were hysterical though, and the Christians also worked against the Emperor. A turning point happened on a Pagan day of festival. On that day, it was said the Christians burned the Temple of Daphne. It caused great sorrow among the Pagans. Julian went into mourning and seclusion. When he was next seen in offices of government the officials wondered at his sanity. Julian exacerbated this by claiming to hear the voices of the Gods themselves, and he took to swatting their whisperings from his ears.

The previously high-minded and innovative Julian gave over to his desire for revenge. His higher virtues were crushed by sadness and anger. His higher virtues were crushed by a madness induced by the thwarting of his religious rituals. Tolerance was set aside and a great tumult erupted. Christians were dragged in the streets, skinned, tasted on spits and tortured to death all in his name. He ordered the sacking of the library of the Christian bishop of Cappadocia. He declared war on Persia and sought his own deification.

It was surprising that this man, who modeled his thinking on the values of philosophers and poets and the rule of Hadrian and Marcus Aurelius, would become sullied by a galloping personal cruelty. He had emphasized government accountability, fairness of decision making, proper and equitable remuneration for services rendered and food and comfort for all. He began with ideals of religious tolerance and it was religion that unglued him in the end.

Many nations recognize the need for separation of church and state. In the matters of healthcare it also seems important that institutions and caregivers exclude religion from care-giving. This is challenging as issues of care and the moral questions that surround choices and options are very foundational questions in most religions.

Finding a formula for dealing with opposing religious values over healthcare including: hands-on care giving, treatment options, ongoing research, birth, death and all in between would be helpful in ensuring the innovative leader isn't cut down in her efforts toward advancing an institution, and isn't rendered incompetent by the sheer emotional content of her own religious beliefs. It would suggest that institutional innovation and religion are incompatible, because, historically, religion has shown itself to turn and bite innovation while corrupting institutional goals.

In the grocery store of politics and healthcare there is no room for religion. Both interests require cool heads that operate the big picture. Religion is notorious for heating up the grey matter, and rapidly accelerates best-before dates. Decomposition of clear thinking sets in fast. Innovation is necessarily religion free and does not need to be refrigerated after opening.

Poor Julian, he just couldn't shed the festering hot Gods.

CONCLUSION

Desire Creation Innovation

Then life was not
Non life was not
No vast expanse of air
Nor vaster realm of sky that lies beyond.
Was water there
The deep abyss of ocean?

Then death was not
Non death was not
No change of day or night
And covering all the gloom was lost in gloom
All was unseen
One universe unknown

Then up rose desire
Fierce glowing desire
The seed of spirit
The germ of mind
The source of life
Begetting mighty forces
All heaved in breathless motion

Who then knows
Who can now declare?
When cometh creation?

He the Primal one
Whose eye controlleth all things
He alone doth know it
Or perhaps even he
Knoweth it not.

This is the Hindu Creation myth of the *Rg Veda*, (the translation which
appears published, undated and uncredited by Masters Music Publications

Inc. of Miami Lakes, Florida) that is presented by the composer Holst. One of the most informative aspects of it, in this herbaceous consideration of innovation, is what happens in the orchestra at a particular moment.

The first two verses are sung without accompaniment until their very last line. Then in tandem in three low octaves the note C is played. The chord is played and held for twenty-four beats. It has the effect of establishing a rumbling drone; an aural foundation. It lands on the mention of a creator; the One.

Rhythmically, the first verses plod as if to show simplicity and near nothingness. Then the foundation lifts. The chord is released. There is silence in the bass-line for three beats. Then there is a bursting of the musical line. It begins in the low tones and pours forth to the upper registers in a great gush of sound. It all happens on one word, desire.

Then up rose desire....

Then up rose is sung without accompaniment and as the downbeat happens on the s of desire, the instrumentation lands and springs up like a fountain. It reaches a flowering peak and descends.

Fierce glowing desire

It is rapturous, sensuous and bountiful.

The seed of spirit
The germ of mind
The source of life,
Begetting mighty forces

There are two quick lines of building intensity, then,

All heaved in restless longing,

the accompaniment anchors and is solid with accented downbeats. The composition is, perhaps, not a sophisticated one but it captivates. The whole collection of songs based on the *Rg Veda*, are obvious.

Some songs have an illustrated children's book quality about them. *Song of the Frogs* is particularly delightful in this respect. The frogs sit around the pond. The music bounces, hops and jumps. An image is created. The narrative brings the rains and the frogs are happy.

Like Brahmins sitting around the altar.
Who gladly talk of holy rite
'round the pond the frogs are singing

The song of *Dawn* , *Ushas*, is an unfolding. It is an awakening. The song of Indra, of battle, is fierce. Even my eight month old child understood it as terrifying as he did Holst's Mars from his symphony *The Planets*. Let's face it, mythology, fairy tales, and even blockbuster novels all pull from simple recipes and are applied to our simple emotional spectrum.

Desire is identified in the ancient text, the Sanskrit of the *Rg Veda*, as the beginning of all things including consciousness. It is yearning. It is identified as essential to the creation of the things we see as primary: spirit, mind and material. The composer identifies this on the downbeat of the s of desire.

The birth of spirit.
The germ of mind.
The force of life.
All heaved in restless longing.

There is no innovation without someone expressing a longing of a kind. It is a yearning that pulls them along. There have always been great swaths of religious and intellectual pilgrims devoted to the culling of desire from the world; cleaning it up, so to speak. Now that's a shame. Sure desire causes all sorts of trouble, as much in the Hindu myths as anywhere else, but the greatness or problem of Us is that we are simple and our palate is limited. Desire moves us toward beauty, truth, wholeness, and it evolves us.

So, what is innovation? It is a product, or function, or process of yearning for a new way. The impressionist painters were innovators in the way they depicted the world. They built a world out of strokes and dabbles and yearning for a vibrant image; perhaps a hyper-real image. Perhaps they were yearning for a new clarity, and that is why each age has its own version of hyper-realism. Each age seeks a new clarity.

Perhaps the reason innovation seems more powerful than newness, is that its life-force is desire, and like energy, desire is active. The energy is deliberate, conscious and exciting.

What is innovation? It's not the image or the result. It is an unfinished energetic attempt to create image, make a whole, or to find a result. I suppose there is something incomplete in the impressionist painting. It requires the viewer to put the pieces together. Maybe that's what makes the work so exciting. It is active.

As I walked, then, around those Healthcare convention halls and wondered about the booths and the displays, the charts and the mind maps, I realize that my curiosity about all the stuff between the lines and the intent in the arrows that join one thought process with another on a Bristol-board display is valid. It suggests to me that a definition for innovation is possible and it is informative. We are at any time shuffling universal values into our personal needs and vice versa, and these weigh upon and come from the institutions in which we engage and the political theatre in which we live.

A look at the picture painted by the coming together of this innovation palette, shows that in the Universal realm there is a constancy of no surprises. Human needs seem to be timeless and they shape everything that follows. Our Particular needs seem to be a microcosm of the universal. However, as the discussion pulls away from the Universal to the Particular and then to the Institutional something begins to reveal itself. I found help in understanding this in my discussions with the Ontario Institute for Cancer research. The key, at least for our times, appears to be method.

If we look back on the Universal and Particular themes, method plays an important role. Within the Universal realm method is about bringing the touchstones of beauty, truth, sustenance and the others into a whole. In the theme of the Particular method is urgently sought as a conscious person attempts to understand self and the world. Within the framework of Institutions method is not only a device that keeps the organization afloat, it is as Dr. Robert Phillips pointed out the key to managing the massive data or change that reigns down upon the organization and in his case, the scientists. It is method that keeps the mandate of the institution in focus. In the Political realm method is perhaps most recently and dramatically discussed in the passing of the Health Reform Act in the United States and the forensic press being applied to the machinations of the White House Chief of Staff, Rahm Emmanuel and Speaker of the House, Nancy Pelosi. Method may not have moved the reform to the end-zone which so many Democrats wanted but it moved that country a step toward it, and that was all achieved through political maneuvering; a very deliberate point by point method. It was method used in an effort to express the values of a particular electorate.

For the opera singer, method allows artistry to come through and it is method that allows for the expression, then, of the artform. It is desire that creates the aesthetic and the need for aesthetic.

In the dowdy and earnest scene of convention hall gatherings a bunch of well-intentioned people of a certain expertise try to get on with their jobs. Some think big and some only about the widget in hand. All are participating in an unspoken decorum or method of interaction. Somehow through leadership, accident or the sheer force of the energy represented by the arrows in the mind maps, innovation will come. If there is yearning in the arrows, innovation will come.

We won't see it but it will suddenly be upon us born of our desire to keep moving toward a beacon. Sure this is an optimistic idea but optimism and desire are somehow wedded just like they are in the mind of a traveler. It's simply part of who we are. Just ask the Colobus monkey and that happy guy Darwin who gave his back to the smiters.

So what is innovation? It is the methodical expression and fleeting near-actualization of our desire. Where do we find it? We find it in our perception of beauty. How do we find beauty? We recognize mistakes and move toward an ideal, a beacon. We embrace risk. We play. We listen. When will we find it? If we stay energized and true, happily, never. We'll just find the path. Why? Because innovation just keeps on trying. Is this useful? It's not immediately apparent, but we are an applied species and we'll make a tool of these notions somehow.

Bibliography

Nien Cheng, *Life and Death in Shanghai*,
Grafton Books, London 1984, ©Nien Cheng 1986
John Dewey, *Experience and Nature*
Dover Publications, Mineola 1958
P. Lain Entralgo, *Doctor and Patient*
World University Library, McGraw-Hill Book Company/© P. Lain
Entralgo1969,
Translation by Frances Partridge/© George Weidenfeld and Nicholson
John Fraser, *The Chinese*
Summit Books, New York, ©1980 John Fraser
Edward Gibbon, *The Decline and Fall of the Roman Empire*
Everyman's Library, Alfred A. Knopf, New York, Toronto 1910
W von Goethe, *Meeres Stille*
(Schubert) 200 *Songs in three volumes*
Volume 1: 100 *Songs*
International Music Company, New York Selected by Sergius Kagen
Robert Graves, *Goodbye to All That*
Anchor Books, London 1929
George Friedrich Handel, Charles Jennens, *Messiah*
Novello Handel Edition, general editor Watkins Shaw/Novello and
Company Limited, London 1742
Richard Holmes, *The Age of Wonder: How the Romantic Generation
Discovered the Beauty and Terror of Science*
Harper Press, London 2008, © Richard Holmes 2008
Gustav Holst, *Vedic Hymns Op 24*
Masters Music Publications, Inc./Miami Lakes, Florida
Thomas Kuhn, *The Structure of Scientific Revolutions*
Chicago University Press 1962
Eric J. Leed, *The Mind of the Traveller: From Gilgamesh to Global Tourism*
Basic Books,A Division of Harper Collins, New York 1991
Nelson Mandela, *Long Walk to Freedom*
Little Brown & Company, 1995
Eugene Rogan, *The Arabs A History*
Basic Books, Perseus Books Group, New York
© 2009 Eugene Rogan

Bertrand Russell, *In Praise of Idleness/Essay* 1932
George Allen & Unwin Limited, London 1935
Simon Schama, *Citizen: A Chronicle of the French Revolution*
First Vintage Books Edition 1990/Divsion of Random House, Inc.,
New York, © 1989 by Simon Schama
Joanna Spyri, Heidi/Thomas Y Crowell Company, 1902
Dawn Starin, *Contemplating Colobus*
Philosophy Now, a magazine of ideas/London, March/April 2009
TED: Ideas Worth Spreading/ www.ted.com
Barbara W. Tuchman, *A Distant Mirror, The Calamitous 14th Century*/
Alfred A. Knopf, New York 1978, © 1978 Barbara W. Tuchman
C. Vann Woodward, *The Burden of Southern History*
Louisiana State University Press, Baton Rouge, © 1960 C. Vann
Woodward
Richard B. Wright, *October*, Harper Collins Publishers Limited
        A Phyllis Bruce Book, 2007

CPSIA information can be obtained at www.ICGtesting.com
Printed in the USA
LVOW042327231012

304133LV00001BA/4/P